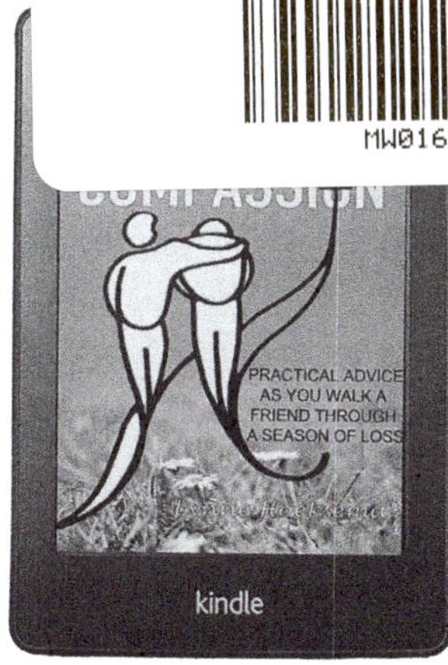

FREE GIFT!

Cultivating Compassion

Amazon Best Selling Book

Feeling ill-equipped to be a natural nurturer is a nearly universal phenomenon. *Cultivating Compassion* can help you break through that awkwardness and become an effective comforter. Here's what you'll find:

- Insights into the emotions of the grieving world
- Practical "now and later" suggestions
- What to say and do, what NOT to say and do - and the "WHYs" behind it
- God's call to be compassionate, and how he can equip you

Check out this FREE PDF to help you overcome all this awkwardness!

You can grab your FREE copy here:

lynnehoeksema.com/cultivating-compassion-ebook

Endorsements

"*The Honest Griever* brings confirmation to readers that there is no right or wrong way to work through their sorrow. Lynne's refreshing words come not from a place of judgment, but from a true desire to help anyone suffering a loss.

"While giving an account of her own experience, she stresses our uniqueness and gives us permission to grieve in our own way. It is refreshing to hear her acknowledge her honest feelings. I appreciate that as Lynne writes about a topic, she also shares the blog posts that were written while experiencing that moment, giving readers a sense of real-time grieving. She doesn't apologize, justify, or belittle herself. Lynne epitomizes an honest griever, demonstrating a healthy and loving relationship with herself, which is exactly what God wants for us all."

—**Angie Lookingbill**, Coach, *Whole-Hearted Living*

"I love reading and writing, with a greater emphasis on reading, more recently. My publishing experience includes many articles and one book. I enjoy the different perspectives others have on many topics, but sensitive topics like grieving have become so much more personal to me as I get older. So this increased sensitivity often makes it difficult to read what others have to say about these topics. The discomfort is noticeable to me, and frankly, not very welcome!

"When I was given the opportunity to read a draft of Lynne's book, I expected to read a women's perspective on grief. And quite honestly, that didn't hold much appeal for me. What I found instead was a book that was almost gender neutral. *The Honest Griever* is not just for women, but shares insights that men can benefit from as well. Oh sure, you can't help but know a woman wrote it, but when you look at the stories, experiences, and opportunities to learn about grief, they apply to all of us. It's about helping others through the grieving process, but it also prepares you for the personal grief that comes from those losses that almost everyone encounters during our lifetime.

"Lynne is a gifted writer. I wish I could write like her. You don't just read her books; you feel them. *The Honest Griever* sinks in your mind, it changes how you act, and it makes you understand grief in a way you never have before."

— **Gary A. Higbee**, International speaker and author of *Inside Out*

"While reading *The Honest Griever*, I felt like I could tell Lynne anything. I so badly wanted to be reading with her sitting across from me with a cup of coffee while I said, "Me too, me too!" Her openness begged for a response from me about my journey as a widow. Lynne has covered it all. She assured me that, I too, am an "honest griever." This is a book you can refer to as needed. Not a one-time read. And as a women's ministries director, *The Honest Griever* will be a tool in my box for needy souls.

— **Judie Colyer**, Director of Women's Ministries, Ankeny (IA) Evangelical Free Church

The Honest Griever

TRUTHS GOD TEACHES ON THE JOURNEY FROM PAIN TO PURPOSE

Lynne Hoeksema

Daisy Publishing

Urbandale, IA 50323

lynnehoeksema.com

Printed in the United States of America

Cover Design by Britney Wilson

Typesetting by Liz Smith - InkSmithEditing.com

ISBN: 978-1-7351828-1-0

Dedication

To my husband, Dale, whose love and support and encouragement throughout our life together helped mold me into the person I am today – a woman who misses you desperately, but who knows that God has called her to share all that she's learned in the process of losing you.

Contents

Acknowledgments

As any author will attest, we don't reach this final product without an army of others encouraging us and lending their talents and gifts to this process.

To all my early readers, thank you for so freely sharing your insights, suggestions, reactions, impressions, and so much more. To those of you with that extra "editor's gene," I'm grateful for the honing skill you gently applied to these words. And for the hours we spent debating! Seriously, it was a joy for me.

Britney Wilson, every time we work on a project, I'm in awe of your graphic design talents. I'm blessed that you've chosen to walk this journey with me, and look forward to many more years of creative collaborations.

I'm grateful to my friends, too many to list here, who encouraged me to keep moving forward, despite discouragement, despite a pandemic, and despite the heartache I was forced to relive again. We crossed this finished line!

Above and through it all, I'm grateful to God, who is not only "the author and perfecter of [my] faith" (Hebrews 12:2 ASV), but the author and perfecter of this story. I look forward to walking with him on *this* journey until the day he calls me home. To God be the glory.

SECTION I

Prelude

"I have told you these things, so that in me you may have peace. In this world you will have trouble. But take heart! I have overcome the world."

– John 16:33 (NIV)

1

Our Story

I don't remember praying. I remember screaming. As a Christian, I thought I would have turned immediately to God The moment I had been dreading most of my life was now here. My husband was dead, and I was walking into uncharted territory. How in the world can that be? I just talked to him three times! I was going to see him this afternoon! Don't tell me he's gone…

The story of how God walked this woman through widowhood is only complete by looking first at the marriage that preceded it. I *love* to talk about my husband, Dale, and the relationship we had for more than three decades. So, if you'll indulge me for a few minutes, I'll share our story.

I met Dale when we both worked for Northwestern Bell, back when the Bell System was still intact. That should give you some idea how long ago it was. Dale was 20 years older than me, had three grown children and, at the time, two grandchildren. Coming from a conservative Christian background, this was not who I thought I would fall head over heels in love with. And trust me, it wasn't exactly what my parents had in mind for their only daughter either!

But he was handsome and witty and charming, and was so void of any pretense, and so full of confidence without being arrogant, that I found myself completely enamored with him. We started dating in the early 80s and our love for each other only grew deeper over time. My mom accepted this relationship relatively quickly (apparently, he charmed her too …), but it was going to take a little longer for my dad!

So we dated for five years which included a transfer for me from the Des Moines area up to the Twin Cities in Minnesota. We survived that separation and Dale was subsequently transferred there about 15 months later. After more than a year-long engagement, we got married September 27, 1986, on the Mississippi River, aboard the Jonathan Padelford Riverboat out of The Port of St. Paul.

We built our first home together north of Stillwater, MN, and so began 27 years of living on acreages in Minnesota and Iowa. As I look back on those years, I can only be grateful for the memories we made during that time and for how God blessed our marriage.

In 1992, after the unexpected death of my dad, we moved from Minnesota back to Iowa where we could be closer to my now-widowed mom and Dale's family. But we didn't give up our country life and once again, were blessed to live on some beautiful acreages.

Our relationship wasn't traditional in any sense of the word. Of course the 20-year age difference set us apart from the get-go. I eventually became a step-grandma to six grandkids and, to date, have added six *great* grandkids to the mix.

We were both quite independent and always felt free to pursue our own hobbies. Dale, at heart, was a biker (not the exercise kind!) and a fisherman. I was much more into music, gardening, and golf. While our interests were different, we were both completely supportive of each other's hobbies. Together we shared a love of the outdoors, a love of animals, and the fun of socializing with friends. If Dale were here today, I think he'd agree that our *favorite* times were our dinner and movie dates – just the two of us.

I think what defined so much of our marriage was this deep love we had for each other that spanned decades. Not too long after we started dating, Dale told me he would always love me. I marveled at how sure he was. I told him that I hoped the same was true for me, but how could you really know *forever*? He said, "I just know." It's a precious memory even today. He will forever be the love of my life.

I remember when Dale went on a two-week mission trip to Brazil about 20 years into our marriage and called me in the middle of the trip because he couldn't go another day without talking to me. I felt the same way: we couldn't go long without making that connection.

I never once doubted Dale's love for me or his faithfulness to me. What an incredible gift that will always be.

That doesn't mean we didn't disagree or have arguments or let selfishness or pride work their way into our lives regularly. You can't have a 35-plus-year relationship and not have some struggles due to our sin nature, if nothing else!

But none of that ever changed the fact that we were committed to our marriage and each other until death do us part.

In 2008 after 22 years of marriage, Dale was diagnosed with vascular dementia and thus began the most difficult season of our marriage. In the early years of this disease, I was likely the only one who noticed the change. He was able to carry on most aspects of his life with just minor interruptions. But over the next few years, his physical health also began to decline and eventually reached the point where he couldn't do the work on the acreage anymore, and I couldn't do it alone.

So in 2013 we made the difficult decision to move off the acreage. Within three days of our move, Dale was hit with a terrible case of shingles which led to multiple ear surgeries and several six-week rounds of daily IV antibiotics. During this time, he also had a GI bleed resulting in too-many-to-count emergency room trips and visits to doctors. Add to that several deaths in my family and numerous other challenges and we had a year like no other.

Dale suffered so much and it wreaked havoc on him physically and mentally. I was exhausted from the stress of his care, on top of working and trying to keep everything running at home. So many times during that first year in town I cried out, "God, I hate this. But I trust you."

After a life that was overwhelmingly idyllic and mostly untainted by deep trials, my faith was now tested by the relentless nature of one crisis after another after another. God taught me that he does indeed walk alongside us during our most difficult days.

The next few years were mostly crisis-free, but now began the slow, painful dementia decline. I grieved every single step down. It was a heartbreaking ritual.

I struggled mightily with this season. I so wanted to be patient throughout, but found myself often asking God to forgive me for *not* being patient. I repeated virtually everything I said to Dale – multiple times. We couldn't enjoy a movie or TV show together because he couldn't follow the story line. Our conversations became shallow and mundane, mostly talking about the weather or what we might have for supper.

As the dementia worsened, so did his judgment and discernment. Because he was always so mechanically minded, he thought he could still get around and fix things. I will never forget the argument we had when our water heater quit working and he wanted to relight it. I knew we had to take some preliminary precautions before trying to light it, but I couldn't convince him of that or stop him.

So, he is down on his hands and knees (no easy feat for him in his feeble condition), trying to get the handheld lighter to ignite. I'm standing there literally praying to God that Dale doesn't blow us both up! I'm convinced it was divine intervention that kept that lighter from firing up! We lived to see another day …

Multiple episodes like this painfully and reluctantly brought me to the conclusion that I couldn't keep Dale safe at home any longer. So, unbeknownst to him, I began the search for a care facility.

I talk more about the amazing way God led me through this search in Chapter 17 but for now, just know that I found a place that was exactly what we both needed.

Once God opened that door, I was *so* afraid to tell Dale what I had been up to and dreaded what his reaction might be. I waited until after his 80th birthday and then sat down across from him. I said, "This is the hardest conversation I'll ever have with you," and immediately began to cry!

As I explained that it would be best for him to live where he could be cared for properly, and that I had found a good place for him with his own room, he said, "I don't want to go." To which I replied, "I know you don't. But I can't keep you safe here at home anymore." His response? "Okay, well if that's what I have to do."

Thank you, Dale, and thank you, God! What a huge relief it was to me that he so graciously accepted this next step in his care.

Not only did he adjust quickly and completely to this new life, but he said it was the right place for him to be for the final 10 months of his life. I couldn't have been more grateful.

One of the biggest blessings of this move was that I could now go from being the sole, full-time caregiver for someone with dementia, to being Dale's wife again. It was an amazing time of restoration for our marriage after such difficult years. We were still able to reminisce about all the wonderful years we'd had together and how blessed we were to have had the relationship we did throughout our marriage. When I asked him if he remembered that early profession of always loving me, he said he did, and that it was still true. Be still, my heart.

On the morning of October 16, 2017, I awoke to the phone ringing at about 5:00 a.m. It was Dale and I was still asleep. I'd love to tell you that I said,

"Hi honey, so nice to hear from you." But what I said instead was, "Dale, why are you calling me so early? I'm still sleeping!" To which he responded, "Oh, okay," and immediately hung up.

About an hour later, he called again. Similar conversation. I told him he didn't need to call again.

But an hour later, at his usual time, the phone rang again. At this point I went through the normal conversation we had every morning when he'd call. "Are you ready for breakfast? Have you taken your medication? Okay, I'll see you this afternoon."

At 9:30 a.m., three of my friends came over for a Monday Bible study. As it was winding down and one of the gals had already left, my land line phone rang around 11:15 a.m. I didn't recognize the number, so I didn't answer. A few seconds later, my cell phone rang with the same number. Hmmm …

But it wasn't the care facility's number or the head nurse's number, so I ignored it again as I was still chatting with my two friends. However, I did take a quick glance at my phone and I now had a "PLEASE CALL ASAP" message in my email.

When I told my friends what it said, they asked if they should stay. I thought it was probably a good idea.

It took what seemed like an eternity to reach the nurse who was filling in for the head nurse that day. He proceeded to explain what had transpired from the moment Dale pulled the call button cord, through the symptoms they were seeing, and the 911 call they made to the paramedics. And then he said, "I'm so sorry, but he passed."

And so "the honest griever" begins her journey.

2

The Aftermath

From the very second my grief descended upon me, God was caring for me. In the most devastating moment of my life, God placed two strong Christian women in my home so I wouldn't be alone when the bottom dropped out of my life.

I called my closest friend, Renae, and tearfully told her that Dale had died. Then my two friends and I headed to the care facility. Even though he was already gone, I knew how important it was for me to go to him in that moment.

Once I was allowed into his room, I sobbed my good-byes to him, wondering how this could possibly be what I was doing. Then my friends and I were taken to a private section of the facility where a police officer was on hand to ask me some routine questions. Right … routine. Since the facility didn't provide full nursing-level care, any death had to be "investigated" to make sure nothing unscrupulous had occurred.

When that was finished, I tackled a task I had long dreaded – calling his three grown children to let them know their dad was gone. Shock, devastation, tears, and on some level, denial. We had it all. And we all had it. One of our grandsons wanted to be with me and came to the care facility, allowing my two friends to get back to their own families.

My phone began ringing and text messages began coming in from my friends. How did they know? As you recall, I told my friend Renae about Dale's death right before we left the house. Here's the next provision from God: a month or two before, I started thinking about what might happen if I died unexpectedly before Dale. He would have no idea who to call! So, I put together a list of people that covered all the basic "friend groups" in my life so Renae could make sure the right people heard about *my* death. (Yes, I'm *that* kind of planner!)

Well, unbeknownst to me, she decided to use that list to let my friends know that Dale had just died, saving me the heart-wrenching job of calling everyone with my tragic news.

My grandson and I were now the only ones left at the care facility and I didn't know why we were still there. The last thing I wanted was to be around when the funeral home came for his body, so we headed back to my house.

Several friends stopped by soon after we arrived, some offering to pick up groceries for the extra visitors coming over the next few days. Some came to give me a hug and share in my devastation. Eventually, everyone went home, and I was left alone. Now what? Gee, I guess I should write his obituary. The family had plans to meet at the funeral home the next afternoon so there was no time to waste.

How many of you are fans of the movie *Steel Magnolias*? It was released in 1989 and had a *great* cast of characters. There's a heartbreaking cemetery scene where the main characters are deeply grieving the death of young Shelby, played by Julia Roberts. It's hard to watch and makes the list of most tearful movie scenes. But what happens next is what I remember *most* about this scene.

At the pinnacle of their grief when Shelby's mother, played by Sally Field, has a complete meltdown, she cries out, "I just want to hit somebody! And I want to hit them hard!" Olympia Dukakis grabs Shirley MacLaine (Louise, aka Ouiser) and says, "Here, hit Ouiser! We can make T-shirts that say, 'I hit Ouiser!'" Everyone, except Ouiser, of course, breaks into fits of laughter. It's one of the best examples I've ever seen of comic relief in the middle of a display of heart-wrenching grief.

This won't come anywhere close to that, but it's my feeble attempt to add a little levity to the sadness of *my* story.

As I began to write Dale's obituary, I was reminded of a conversation we had a few months before he went to the care facility. We were talking about end-of-life planning, and specifically his obituary. Remember that he had had dementia for about eight years at this point. He said to me, "How are you going to write my obituary? You don't know anything about me."

I burst into laughter! I said, "Seriously? I've been with you for 35 years and you don't think I know anything about you?" He proceeded to ask me a slew of questions, "Did you know this…?" "Yes." "Did you know this…?" "Yes."

And so it went until he was finally convinced that maybe his wife of 31 years really did know a few things about him. It makes me laugh even today.

I finished the obituary, including all the events and activities he wanted to make sure I knew about him. And off to bed I went. Not to sleep, however. Sleep wouldn't come for another 24 hours.

The next morning began the onslaught that is inherent after any death, it seems. People calling, stopping by with food and supplies. Family making plans to fly into Des Moines. Funeral home meeting to finalize the details we hadn't already decided upon. Dale and I had done most of the pre-funeral planning already. It's a *huge* relief to have so much of that completed ahead of time, and alleviates a ton of decisions the family won't have to make during a confusing, foggy time.

The next few days were spent going through photographs with Dale's kids, trying to decide which ones to include in the video. I worked on music for the service and all the minutiae that goes into planning a visitation and funeral. Mostly we were just on autopilot.

Even though I had seen Dale declining, probably more clearly than anyone in his life, I was still completely taken by surprise at his death. So you can imagine the shock that his kids and grandkids were struggling with.

We survived the week. We were blessed by so many who came to offer their condolences to us and show kindness in so many ways. We had one final family brunch on Sunday after the services. Then everyone went back to their homes and their broken lives to figure out how to live without this man we all loved so dearly.

Deep in my soul, I knew my life would never be the same again. I am now the grieving widow at age 60. I have no parents and no biological children of my own. I felt *very* alone. I was now entering the season of my life where my greatest strength and comfort would come from God. I would need to lean on him more fully than I ever had in my life.

But this was always intended to be God's plan, and at this time. In Psalm 139:16, it says, "Your eyes saw my unformed substance; **in your book were written, every one of them, the days that were formed for me, when as yet there was none of them"** (emphasis mine). I knew that God had determined the exact moment of Dale's death since before he was even born. I take *great* comfort in that. There is *zero* randomness about his death. I trust a good God. And I would learn through great pain exactly what that would entail. I hope you, too, can find comfort in this verse during whatever trial you're enduring. It speaks directly to the intimate, and yet sovereign character of God.

I want to share one final, critical revelation before I conclude with a couple of blog posts. During those last few years when my life was filled with handling one crisis after another, followed by years of caring for "an old man with dementia," I struggled with what felt like the loss of the one-of-a-kind love that I had for Dale. I remember the first time admitting to a friend, "I won't miss these days," and feeling guilty for saying it. I still had my husband, but there was virtually no joy in this part of the journey.

For many of those days, I said, "I can't do this one more day." And yet, I did, for years. It wreaked havoc on our relationship and I seriously wondered if I even loved him anymore, which was one of the saddest thoughts of my life.

And then Dale died. And grief and heartache and devastation overwhelmed me. As I write these words, 29 months after Dale's death, I am sobbing at the memory of that pain.

You know what that tells me? Of course, I still loved him. Deeply. And forever.

This pain that is always hiding just under the surface is proof positive that my love for Dale never disappeared. It was just buried under layer after layer of difficulties during those last years. What I know to be true without a doubt is this: DEEP LOVE = DEEP GRIEF. If you're grieving deeply, know that it is the price you pay for being blessed with a profound love.

It's why I still cry two and a half years after becoming a widow. A double-edged sword, for sure.

I purposely gave this amount of space and time to our story because it absolutely informs everything else I experienced after Dale's death. It's important for you to know what kind of relationship we had, both in the good times and in the hard times. Every moment of my life with Dale feeds into my journey through widowhood.

My journey is unique. You'll hear me talk about that often. Your journey is unique, too. And yet, it is my prayer that the truths I've come to embrace along this journey can also give you hope and a greater, clearer picture of the God who loves us and walks every step of our journeys with us.

And so "the honest griever" says her earthly good-bye.

For about 20 months, I chronicled that journey on my first blog site, *It's Beyond Me*. Most of the nearly 50 posts were heart-wrenching for me to write and brought on a flood of tears. And ironically, much healing.

I have chosen to make those posts an integral part of this book. So, why not just write the story from my three-year rearview mirror? Why was it important to find a home for these posts? Because I want the perspective to be in "real time." I want you to know that *this* is how I felt at the six-month and twelve-month and two-year anniversaries of Dale's death. I want you to get a glimpse into what wedding anniversaries feel like to a widow. I want you to experience the wonder of new scripture revelations with me, the day I received them. I want you to be in awe along with me when God shows himself to me in surprising ways.

I pray that you'll be able to step into some of these experiences and glean wisdom for your own sake, and for whatever trial in which you may be struggling.

You'll see a number below the title of each blog post. It identifies how many days had passed since Dale's death, at the time of the writing.

You will find certain stories or perspectives repeated in multiple posts. I leave them in despite their repetition, to emphasize whatever point I felt important enough to say more than once. I thank you in advance for tolerating the duplications!

And, truth be told, I don't completely trust my memory. You and I would both miss some of the power of the moments if I just wrote what I remember today. So infusing these real-time writings into the heart of this book will give you a front row seat on the journey with me.

I wrote a couple of blog posts after Dale's death that looked at some common misconceptions about losing a loved one. These were written within the first year and a half after his death when my emotions were still raw. I hope they give you the insights I had to learn the hard way.

"Can You Really Prepare to Lose a Loved One?"

Day 316

In a recent conversation with a friend, she told me how Dale's death and the death of another friend's spouse had caused her and her husband to take a serious look at what lie ahead for them. They are understanding more and more the inevitability that *one* of them will be grieving the loss of the other. And they were preparing themselves for that sad day, sometime in the future.

I found myself in a similar frame of mind in the weeks before Dale died. I could clearly see that he was declining both physically and mentally. And given the fact that no one in his immediate family had lived longer than age 81 (he was 80 at the time), I didn't have many illusions about a long life ahead for him.

In fact, we had a conversation just a few weeks before he died where I told him, "I'm preparing to lose you sometime in the next year." How crazy is that? But it was absolutely my thinking at the time and there was no one I shared more of my thoughts or hopes ... or fears with more than I did with Dale. So, it made sense that I would share this as well.

He was not offended by it and took it in the spirit it was intended – I wanted him to know that I was struggling to figure out how I could make it through this great loss that was likely not far out on the horizon. It led to a discussion confirming that he was ready to go and he knew he was going to heaven. I think we both took great comfort in the whole conversation.

Then, long before that magic "preparation" year had passed, that fateful Monday morning in October arrived and answered the title question. Can you really prepare to lose a loved one? For me, the answer was clear. You. Can. Not.

No amount of mental preparation equipped me for the onslaught of emotions that hit me from the second I heard the words, "He passed," up to today when I still grieve this loss so very deeply.

Oh sure, you might be able to take some of the "surprise" factor out of the equation. And certainly you can and should do the legal preparation for someone's death. Have the will or trust, power of attorney (medical and financial), and living will documents in place, so you don't have the added stress of dealing with those issues. You can even go so far, as Dale and I did, to plan and pay for your funeral ahead of time. All good things that I highly recommend.

But was I emotionally prepared for Dale's death? Absolutely not. If you've been following along with any of my previous posts, you know how deep this pain still is and how long it is likely to last. In some manner, forever.

No amount of planning or preparation on my part gave me any kind of "head start" in the grieving process. It is what it is, and you must work through it one painful day at a time.

So, do I have any words of encouragement for you, my readers? I absolutely do! Say and do the things *today* that your heart, or the Holy Spirit, is telling you to. Make the apologies that are due. Say the "I love yous" that someone needs to hear. Mend a broken fence. Forgive. Reach out. Encourage. Witness to. Spend time with. The possibilities are truly limitless and will pay off in huge rewards.

Anything that could become a regret after a loved one's death, can be turned into a precious memory if you act upon it now.

About the same time Dale and I had the "preparing-to-lose-you" conversation, we had another one that is even more comforting to me. I asked Dale to forgive me for the times I wasn't as patient as I should have been – especially during the difficult dementia days. To which he replied, "I already have." How powerful ... and comforting is that?? It speaks volumes about the man he was and why he was so very loved by so many. And it's just a small piece of what I miss so much.

My challenge to you – ask God to lay on your heart the areas or relationships that need mending, or encouragement. And then resolve to act.

I will be praying for an open heart and for boldness to step out in faith. And for the rewards of your obedience to bless you for years to come!

"If possible, so far as it depends on you, live peaceably with all."
–Romans 12:18

"Let no corrupting talk come out of your mouths, but only such as is good for building up, as fits the occasion, that it may give grace to those who hear."
–Ephesians 4:29

"Before and After Grief – the Long Good-Bye"

Day 526

I want to look at two different kinds of grief and how they may or may not overlap. Maybe you've experienced this yourself; maybe you've been an observer and wondered just how to interact in these situations.

I'm talking about anyone who has struggled through the heartbreak of losing a loved one a little bit at a time. Maybe it was because of Alzheimer's or another form of dementia; maybe it was the long, drawn-out pain of dying from cancer; maybe it was a chronic illness or disability that eventually led to their death.

Regardless of how you lose them, the pain is real and deep and often lasts for years. I experienced this first with my mom who died in 2008. Fortunately, she didn't forget who people were, but she struggled with so much confusion and anxiety as the disease progressed. I watched my brilliant mom, who graduated at age 16 with straight A's, struggle with even the simplest of tasks. It broke my heart.

Ironically, the year she died was also the year that Dale was diagnosed with vascular dementia – and so my next journey with this horrible disease began. But this was so much more "in-my-face" since it was my husband of 22 years at that point, and the man I'd loved most of my adult life.

In those last painful years, it felt like life was just a series of steps downward and I grieved every one of them. Every time there was one more thing that Dale couldn't do any more, or couldn't comprehend any more, or couldn't enjoy any more, my heart broke a little more.

It became a very predictable pattern – take a step down, grieve that loss, "accept" that new normal, wait for the next step down. Repeat until the end.

So, here's the real crux of this situation, and the question we must ask. Does losing your loved one a little bit at a time make the grief over their eventual death any less? For me, and for the countless others I've talked with about this, the answer is a resounding, "NO!"

But I completely understand why one might expect that. I wondered that myself. And I must admit, there was a part of me that actually *hoped* I had grieved most of what I had lost of Dale so that his actual death wouldn't be so hard.

Admittedly, there can certainly be an element of relief that someone's pain – either physical or mental – is now over. And I believe that can be a legitimate source of comfort.

As an observer, you might see this as a reason why someone's grieving might not be so deep. Or maybe the loved one who died was older, and that's another reason why the pain or loss should be less. In my case, I had both. And yet neither circumstance lessened my grieving.

Honestly, I was shocked by the length and depth of the pain I felt upon Dale's death and continue to struggle with, despite all the grieving I had done for the years prior to it.

I've tried to analyze that a bit, to figure out why before *and* after grief must exist. I don't have any good answers. They were different, but they were both grieving. I know that I'm still living it. I don't feel that the heartache I'm going through now was lessened one bit by the grieving I did for years before Dale died. It's essentially like grieving *two* deaths ...

SECTION II

The Daily Grind

In this section, I chronicle the realities of day-to-day struggles, the myriad of issues to work through, and the rollercoaster ride that life becomes. But there are blessings sprinkled throughout – and I hope and pray you see what I like to call my "nuggets from heaven."

You'll find an abundance of blog posts from these days, chronicling the essence of what I was experiencing. I can't come close to illustrating these realities now as well as I did while I was walking through them, so I hope the posts can provide the helpful real-time perspective. They will be topical, not chronological so don't try to make sense of any timeline! Honestly, even if they *were* in chronological order, it wouldn't look like a timeline since that is the nature of grieving.

Whether you're grieving through your own loss right now or looking for insights into the process because of a friend or loved one, I hope you find practical suggestions that can speak into your situation.

3

Making Decisions

Popular wisdom advises that we wait at least a year before making any major decisions. I think in general that's a reasonable suggestion, with lots of room for grace before or after of that one-year mark.

Sheer Volume

First, you will be inundated with decisions that need to be made, beginning with the visitation and funeral planning we talked about in the last section. Even though Dale and I had made most of the major decisions regarding our end-of-life events, it was still overwhelming. And I was used to making most of the decisions for the last several years as Dale's dementia worsened. I also had over 20 years of corporate experience that required daily decision making.

Despite all of that, I was overwhelmed with all that needed to be decided as I stepped into this world of widowhood. I can't imagine how hard it would be for someone who didn't have my history. If you're reading this and have none of that previous experience, I would encourage you to find either family members or trusted friends who can help you through the maze of choices you'll need to make. Take it slowly, if necessary. Learn to prioritize what needs to be done *today*. Take a nap if it becomes too much!

I was working from home on contract in the insurance industry during this time and the biggest project of the entire year was due the day of Dale's visitation. I planned to start working on it the Monday he died. Best laid plans …

But that meant I had to jump back into work *immediately*. The out-of-state family members left on Sunday after the weekend services, and I started making phone calls first thing Monday morning – insurance companies, Social

Security administration, Dale's pension department, etc. As soon as I made the initial contacts, I headed to my home office and tried to focus long enough to tackle this major project.

I remember working for a couple of hours at a time and then feeling like a huge tidal wave of grief was building up behind the dam. I'd have to stop and have a good cry to relieve that pressure before I could go back and work another couple of hours.

Give yourself the space to cry and grieve. Take a break when the day becomes overwhelming. There is much healing through our tears.

Over the next few months, I would make some life-changing decisions. I share how God gave me the clearest calling of my life and look at how you, too, can actively seek after God's will in your own situation.

Ministry Calling

A few months after Dale's death, a friend suggested that I process this loss by writing through it. News flash. I'm not a writer! My background is math and finance and that's what most of my corporate jobs entailed. But people did tell me I wrote a decent Christmas letter each year, so I had that!

I debated how to approach this writing idea and soon landed on the option of writing a personal blog. After Googling "How to Start a Blog," I took the plunge and my personal blog, *It's Beyond Me* was born. It was my way of processing through this difficult season.

During those first months after Dale's death, I began to experience what virtually all widows and widowers do – friends who didn't know what to do with me. I'll address this in greater detail in Chapter 6 on Friendship. As someone who also seldom knew what to say or do around someone going through a loss, I now had a completely different perspective.

My second post on the blog was entitled, "What Your Grieving Friend Wants You to Know." The desire to educate others about what is helpful, and what isn't, started to grow in me as I realized what a huge gap existed in this area. Soon after that post, I had coffee with my pastor who said to me, "Lynne, I think you have a ministry here." To which I responded, "I'm afraid you may be right!"

I was simultaneously terrified and energized by this idea! Within a couple of months of the blog debut, and six months after Dale's death, I quit my part-time job to jump into this new venture with both feet. Yikes! But, again, it's the clearest calling from God I've ever experienced and I knew it was the right decision. God made *this* ministry the desire of my heart.

But this chapter isn't about my ministry; it's about decision making. And my process regarding this new direction is different than anything I've ever encountered. I don't want to create the illusion that all decisions will be that crystal clear. None of mine had been up to that point in my life.

It's very possible, and even likely, that the decisions you face won't have a crystal-clear answer. Be patient. And keep reading!

Lessons Learned

I want to share a few lessons learned over the past few years about decision-making that I hope are helpful to you.

First, I don't think the one-year rule is hard and fast. It's more like a one-year suggestion. The basic premise of waiting a year before making major decisions is still solid. A major loss in one's life, like that of a spouse, is devastating. It affects every nook and cranny of your life and your psyche. Our brains are fighting fog daily. We experience first-hand what it means to have "widow brain!" There is good reason to find some level of "new normalcy" before throwing more chaos into your life.

Any loss you're struggling through can have the same effect on the way you process life. If your world is turned upside-down for *any* reason, many of these suggestions may still apply.

That said, God is *not* on the one-year schedule. Through much prayer and conversations with other friends, and searching my *own* heart, despite some of that aforementioned terror, I knew that *this* ministry was what God wanted for me at this time in my life. The amount of time that had passed didn't play into it.

God is on *his* schedule, regardless of what the world tells us, and that's what really matters when making big decisions. Maybe he wants you to wait *three* years before making a big move. Maybe he says, "Go now." How to know?

Granted, it isn't always easy. God doesn't always make his will crystal clear to us. But there are basic steps to take to try and discern his will. One of my favorite Bible studies is Henry Blackaby's, *Experiencing God* (King, Blackaby & Blackaby, B&H Publishing, 2008). He suggests five areas where God can work to help us see his direction more clearly.

1. Scripture
2. Prayer
3. Holy Spirit
4. People
5. Circumstances

In short, ask the Holy Spirit to guide you through scripture texts that speak into your situation. Spend time in prayer and use the wise counsel of believers who are also guided by the Holy Spirit. Then keep your eyes and heart attuned to see God directing. If it's not clear, then wait until the fog lifts a bit.

I have often been caught up in the fear that, if I didn't make exactly the right decision in God's will, my life would be messed up forever more. Now, I'm not giving you permission to make rash decisions, but I believe we can *not* completely blow up our life by a "wrong" decision during this season. We aren't that powerful.

Yes, pray. Yes, seek counsel from other godly people. Yes, look to see if God is showing you an open door. But, if a decision must be made and you don't have clear-cut direction, do the best you can with the information you have at the time. Then trust that God will honor your *desire* to do the right thing, and protect you from completely ruining your life!

There's one more lesson I've learned the hard way, of course, about decision-making. Sometimes we must be *moving* for God to change our direction. Several times while launching the ministry, I literally and figuratively sat and waited for God to clearly open a door. And on all those occasions, God reminded me of a scripture verse from Joshua 3:13.

"And when the soles of the feet of the priests bearing the ark of the Lord, the Lord of all the earth, shall rest in the waters of the Jordan, the waters of the Jordan shall be cut off from flowing, and the waters coming down from above shall stand in one heap."

Did you see what God required of his people? The soles of the priests' shoes had to "rest in the waters of the Jordan" *before* God parted the river! Of course, there are times we rest, waiting for a clearer leading from him. But sometimes, we too must dip our toes in *our* Jordan River and step out in faith, trusting that this same God will move on our behalf as he sees our obedience.

And so "the honest griever" is called by God to her ministry.

4

Back Into the World

Re-entry Timetable

The timing for getting back into a routine again (as if anything will ever be routine again …) will be as varied as the personalities. Some people, like myself, immediately dove back into the work routine. I didn't have much choice, but I think I would have started working right away even if that big project hadn't been looming. I have other widow friends who've done the same thing. If there's now nobody in the house with them, they couldn't bear to be there alone. So work became a reprieve from the empty house.

Others need time to deal with those decisions we just talked through. There is a *lot* of work involved with losing a spouse. The paperwork alone can be daunting. You may still have family in town who want to help you work through these immediate issues. Maybe you know that you can't step back into the world you had before your loss just yet. Let's not overlook the fact that grieving is *exhausting*! If your previous world required a lot of stamina or concentration, it's very possible that you now have very little of either. Staying home for a time may be your best option.

You'll hear this theme again and again throughout the book. *Everyone's journey is unique*. Grieve how *you* need to, not how you see someone else doing it. Or how someone else thinks you should do it. By the way, what you observe in another griever may be far from the reality of that person's grief.

So the decision to step back into your routine sooner or later is primarily your call. Obligations or work requirements may dictate your return date, but be mindful of your energy level and recharge as necessary.

Putting yourself back into the world after a devastating loss is complicated at best. There's no straight trajectory. Some areas of your life may be easier to rejoin. Others may never be the same again. The relationships in your life, whether they be family or friends, will play a major role in how this re-entry happens. And of course, there's no handbook to show you exactly how to do this. Even if you have friends who have been on a similar journey, yours will not be the same.

Their "Stuff"

The other area of "clean-up" that varies widely from individual to individual is that of working through your loved one's personal effects. Some need to deal with it immediately; others virtually never do. My husband's mother passed away from cancer when she was just 68 years old. His dad died when he was 81, so he lived in their home for many years by himself.

After his dad's death, when Dale and his siblings were cleaning out the house, they found that *none* of their mom's belongings had been touched. There was even hair in her hairbrush after 13 years. Clearly their dad had chosen to deal (or not deal) with his wife's death by leaving everything as it was while she was still living. Again, his call whether we agree or not.

I found myself on the other end of that spectrum. I had a bit of a head start on a lot of Dale's "stuff." When he moved to the assisted living facility, we took that opportunity to go through his clothing and many of his other personal items *before* the move. So we weeded out much of what he didn't want anymore, and I did some extra shopping to fill in some gaps left from the purging. His side of the closet and his dresser drawers were empty when he moved.

After he died, I went to his room at the care facility to bring back the remaining wardrobe. In comparison to where we started, it was completely manageable, even in my mental condition. I took a deep breath, laundered everything, packed it in large garbage bags and said "yes" to the friend who offered to take them to a local thrift shop. Done deal. It felt good to have that piece of the gut-wrenching work behind me. However, it would be more than a year before I could get up the courage to work through all the items in his office area. To each their own. You decide.

Choose Your Activities Wisely

Some of this "life re-entry" will happen naturally as you return to work or school or care of your family. Hopefully, some of your friends will stay connected and gently return you to some semblance of a social life. In other cases, you will make deliberate decisions as to when it happens.

In the first few weeks after Dale's death, I returned to church services. I was on the worship team once a month but wasn't ready to be on stage in front of the congregation initially. Music is so powerful that I spent many a worship time crying through the songs. I didn't want that to be on display.

I also also play the piano for the middle and high school choruses in our former small town. Of course, there was a concert scheduled for the same day as Dale's visitation. I'm grateful for the accompanist who stepped in for me at the last minute.

When December rolled around, the music director asked if I wanted to play for their winter concert. I decided to add that activity, which brings me great joy, back into my routine. I told her that I needed some music in my life again.

Social activity for me was hit and miss. Sometimes I could go out with a friend or two. Other times, I was having such a bad day that I couldn't pull myself together. What I found most helpful was when a friend offered to bring a meal to my house and share it with me. That way I could still enjoy their company and great food, but could also have a meltdown in the privacy of my own home if that's what I needed.

Your own re-entry will be tailored to your lifestyle, your personality, your grieving process, and any number of other factors. Don't feel that you must fit into a prescribed pattern. This is *your* journey.

I'd like to close out this chapter with a few blog posts from those months when I was trying to navigate this new world, and trying to figure out just how to get "back into the world."

This first post addresses a very practical dilemma or two that we all will likely face, regardless of the nature of our trial.

"The 'How Are You Doing' Dilemma(s)"

Day 158

This post topic was originally going to be a singular dilemma, not two. But a recent conversation with a friend caused me to tweak that a bit and write about *two* dilemmas - one for me and one for you! How generous of me.

I'll start with my initial inspiration for this article. In an earlier post, I talked about how encouraging it was for me when people check in with me and ask me, "How are you doing? (HAYD) . And while I'm not reneging on that statement, I am finding that I've created a dilemma for myself.

Simply stated, I don't know how to answer that question! It depends on who is asking, how well I know them, what communication means they're using, how much time they have, what kind of day I'm having, and any number of other factors.

Now we've all met acquaintances "on the street" who, upon having the "how are you doing" (HAYD) question posed to them, go on and on with a litany of every little detail of their amazing or pitiful life! Our intention was just a friendly howdy do.

In those first couple of seconds after the question is posed to me, I make a quick determination as to what an appropriate level of detail in my answer should be. If the person is truly just an acquaintance and may not even know that Dale has passed away, or we are just passing each other at church, my obvious answer is, "Good. How are you?"

On the other end of the "HAYD" spectrum are the people who ask me, "How are you doing...really?" Then it's clear to me that they are looking for the nitty gritty of my heart condition and what I'm currently feeling or struggling with. I feel comfortable sharing the grief and pain because I know they genuinely want to know, and apparently have time for it.

In the fuzzy middle are the situations where I struggle to know just how to answer. These are people who know of my loss and would be considered friends. But I'm not necessarily sure how much time they have, if texting limits my answer, or if they really want all the gory details. So far, I've come up with a few semi-noncommittal statements such as, "One day at a time," "I'm hanging in there," "It's still hard," or any number of other pat statements. I'd like to say that God has hit me with his perfect, lightning bolt answer to HAYD, but alas, nothing popped into my head. So, I'll just have to continue muddling my way through this middle fog!

One answer I never give is, "Great!" Two reasons for that – I generally don't feel great. And I don't want to perpetuate the myth that you can recover from a devastating loss like this in just a few months.

Just a side note here - by God's grace, I *am* still able to find blessings in each day through people and events he places in my life. And his promises are still rock-solid to me, so there is still joy in my life. As James so clearly states, "Count it all joy, my brothers, when you meet trials of various kinds, for you know that the testing of your faith produces steadfastness" (James 1:2).

Now onto *your* dilemma! Boy, I'm not sure I even know how to tackle this one. The dilemma is – what *should* you be asking me? Is it, "How are you doing?" Maybe. Or any other number of discussion-opening statements. Again, I'd love to have a lightning-bolt answer from God to tell you how you should communicate with someone who is grieving.

The best I can do for you here is share the helpful questions friends have posed to me in the past five months, with the caveat that they won't be the same for everyone. No wonder this is such a tough subject!

I'm actually fine with the HAYD question, especially with the "*really*" attached to the end. I've also appreciated, "How is your day going?"; "How can I pray for you?"; "What are you struggling with today?"; and "Let's set a date to have lunch/dinner/movie together."

More important than the words you or I use, is the heart from which they come. When a friend clearly wants to know how I'm doing, I sense that, and it really doesn't matter *what* words they use.

While I really did want this post to be much more instructional than it turned out, maybe the message is that there is no one right way to do this – on your end or mine. Trust your instincts or the nudging of the Holy Spirit to guide you on this. And I will strive to do that same with my answers!

I recently had a conversation with a friend who provided me with that "magic bullet" answer I was hoping to share in this previous post. When she told me about it, I immediately knew it had to be included in the book, because it's such a perfect solution to the HAYD dilemma.

She suggests "grading" your day in response to anyone's inquiry. Hence this conversation – "How are you doing?" "I'm having a C- day, today. How about you?" It can be said with a smile on your face which accomplishes two things. It lets your inquirer know quite succinctly how your day is going, and it can be done without getting all sad and mopey. Everyone knows the difference between an A day and a C day!

In this next post, I address an elephant that had unexpectedly shown up in the middle of my room!

"Depression, Grieving ... and Medication"

Day 219

Well, if that title isn't enough to cause an uproar ... or trepidation on my part! I've had a couple of blog post ideas floating around the past few days, but nothing that I felt strongly about running with. In the past 24 hours, I've read certain articles and had several discussions with friends about this topic and then came that overwhelming sense when I know what the next post will be. But this time, I thought, "Boy, I do *not* want to tackle this subject. I don't see an upside and I'm quite sure I will offend people that I love and respect!" I'll just have to trust God for the upside!

So here I am, typing up this explosive topic – mind you, not before praying and asking God to give me *his* words. I do pray that God would help me be clear in what I sense him asking me to share, and that he would give all the readers an open mind and a heart of grace.

So here goes. Let me begin by saying that I have never had to deal with any kind of long-term clinical depression and for that, I'm extremely grateful. Nor have I really walked closely with someone dealing with that horrible disease. I do, however, have friends who have dealt with this and several close friends who have spent decades walking through this nightmare with their loved ones.

I can't even begin to comprehend what it must be like to deal with clinical depression personally, or to watch a loved one suffer through this. My heart breaks for them. Clearly these are the situations where modern medicine can and should step in to help deal with the chemical imbalance wreaking havoc on their brains. I do know many people have found some sense of healing or relief under their doctor's supervision. I also know that healing doesn't always come, and the pain and hopelessness continue.

If any of this describes you or someone you love, please know that my heart goes out to you as you struggle through this very real, very physical challenge.

That, however, is not what I'm experiencing as I grieve the loss of my husband. Yes, I am sad, and I still cry daily, and I'm often overwhelmed by the loneliness. But I feel that I do a disservice to those suffering from clinical depression if I think it's okay to say our sufferings are comparable. Or to put them in the same medical basket.

One thing we do have in common, however, is that the "solution" for either of us is not to just get over it. Society may tell us to think positive thoughts and stop being so blue. Wrong answer – wrong suggestion. Neither suffering benefits from that advice. Clinical depression likely will need medical intervention. Grieving must run its painful course.

Some in the field call my particular grieving a form of situational depression – a sadness borne of some great loss which, theoretically will lessen over time with or without medical help. And maybe that is what I'm dealing with.

Enter the gray area where there is no right or wrong, but only what an individual feels works best for him or her. I have close friends who have benefitted from medication to help them through some exceedingly difficult and stressful times. I supported their decision to do so 100%. It's absolutely their call, and I know that they received relief. No judgment on my part. Grateful when they came out of their self-described fog.

Over the past seven months, friends have suggested to me that I consider taking some medication as well, to help me through these dark days. I know, without a doubt, they had my best interests at heart. They don't want to see me hurting, and feel helpless to know what to do for me. I *love* the heart of those friends who want my pain to go away. But that's not really how grieving works. If it were, I guess it wouldn't be called grieving!

As I explain how and why I came to the decision I made, I hope that you will also extend grace to me and not judge this personal choice I'm embracing. When I engage in conversation with those suggesting

I take some medication, I can honestly tell them that I'm functioning. I exercise daily, I'm sleeping quite well, I'm eating well (actually too much chocolate). I'm not without hope, I'm not suicidal. *I'm grieving!* This is what it looks like. I would even go so far as to say that I don't consider this to be situational depression. It's the process any of us must go through when we grieve the loss of someone we love. Not grieving means you'll pay the price in some other way at some point in your life.

I talked in an earlier post about how God does his best and most permanent work in our lives through our most difficult times. I believe that with my whole heart as I've seen time and time again the lessons God is teaching me as he walks through this journey with me. Some I would never have learned any other way.

So the next lesson came in the form of a question God seemed to be asking of me: "If he does in fact teach me the most through my pain, why would I want to limit what he is going to do in my life by purposely lessening that pain?" I'm not trying to be a martyr here; I'm just trying to be true to where I believe God is leading me on this issue. And possibly share a perspective that you might not have considered before. I certainly didn't have any clue about this until recently!

Let me be clear, this is my path and decision. It's where God is leading me. I don't know where he has, or is, or may lead you down the road. It may very well be to help you through some dark days with effective and trusted medication. And maybe I'll be there some day, too. But right now, this is where he has me.

I make no judgments on anyone choosing medication or procedures for any part of their healing. And I ask that you not judge me for choosing not to go that route. May God give us *all* the grace and understanding to support each other no matter which path we are on!

I mentioned earlier that this path back into the world is not a straight trajectory. This next post looks at the roller coaster ride that so often defines the world of the griever. I'm guessing many of you can relate.

"Roller Coaster Lessons"

Day 427

Over the past few weeks, I've been on a steep roller coaster ride. And I've thought there were worthy blog post topics at the peaks and the valleys. But just when it seemed the time was right to put pen to paper, so to speak, the ride would change directions and either plunge me down or lift me up, and the writing just didn't happen.

I'm sure I'm committing a cardinal sin of blog-writing, but I've decided to combine it all into one blog post. I think there is a lesson, not only in the peaks and valleys, but also in the whole ride.

So, buckle up – we're going to start at the top!

As many of you have probably seen, I recently launched the ministry site – *Be a Blessing to Your Grieving Friend* (at lynnehoeksema.com). A lot of behind-the-scenes work went into preparing for that and it was such a blessing to see it come together earlier this month. I'm excited to see how God will use the ministry for his purposes. Definitely a top-of-the-coaster event.

Then, of course, there's the expected let-down after a big event. Not a huge dip on the ride, but one of those partial hills. You know the kind.

I had coffee this week with a friend who also has a ministry and we were both looking at some down time with nothing on our schedules. No presentations or interviews to prepare for.

She planned to spend this break in her schedule by studying God's Word and drawing closer to him. I thought that was such a meaningful way to fill up what could have been wasted time.

It reminded me of a devotional I read several months ago that has stayed with me, partially because it has a musical theme, but also because it's very insightful. The author talked about how important the rests are in a musical composition. Whether it's a solo piece or a full orchestra composition, the rests are integral to the making of the music. It could be a short sixteenth note rest, or 32 measures of rest if you happen to be the timpani player in an orchestra!

But without them, there is no color, there is no depth, there is no rhythm, there really is no song. That's one of the reasons that God wants us to also take the appropriate rests in our lives. (Or allow him to place them there!) Especially hard to do this time of year, but I'm sure you'd all agree that it's vitally important to maintain any semblance of sanity. Don't look at these times of rest as an interruption to your life, but as a way to bring more beauty to it.

So, now we've just coasted for a little while. What could be next? For me, it was a deep plunge down.

This past week has been extremely difficult. I'm sure that's partially due to the upcoming holiday. Both of my parents died right around Christmas so there's always some melancholy associated with that.

I also received some difficult health news from a good friend this week and got some semi-bad health news for myself the next day.

But what really sent me down to the valley were the two days when I spent hours going through a lot of Dale's personal items. Every time I went downstairs, it just made me sad because that's where his office was and all his stuff. I knew I had to deal with it at some point and since I didn't have much on the schedule, I decided to go for it.

Of course, much of it made me smile, and there was a *lot* of memory-lane strolling. So many items I didn't even know he had kept. For example, he still had his very first pay stub from Northwestern Bell from February 18, 1956! I'm keeping it, too. And five envelopes of his high school graduation announcements. I don't even have any of my own!

But the hardest part of this project was that the totality of all the things I went through was such an overwhelming reminder of everything that made Dale who he was. A folder full of jokes that illustrated his great sense of humor. Job evaluations that highlighted why he was so often their "go to" guy to handle problem situations and people. Books and articles that covered everything mechanical – no wonder he knew how to make or fix anything. Photos that showed his love for his friends and family. And so very much more.

The stark contrast of all these reminders with the reality that he is never coming back just felt like a body slam. I was in tears for so much of this past week and missing him deeply.

This was truly the very bottom of the coaster ride. On Saturday morning I literally cried out to God to bring something into my life that would bless me in this sorrow. I was so emotionally spent and so tired of the tears.

The night before, I had signed up for a free webinar on how to find places to do public speaking. I thought it might be handy information and had set it up for 10:00 a.m. Saturday morning.

So, I dried my tears and opened my laptop for the webinar. It was put on by a man who is currently a professional speaker, but used to be a youth pastor. Extra points for that! In the hour or so of the webinar, he shared some great information and helpful tips. But, as these things always play out, the real meat of this subject could be found in his on-line training classes which were *not* free.

But the detailed information covered there was exactly what I needed for this next step in the ministry; finding the right places to bring this message of blessing those who are hurting. I also never want to be "taken" by a sales pitch, so I didn't immediately purchase the class. But I must admit I was really excited about what this could mean for the ministry.

I actually went to my Bible app and did four different studies on finding God's will! Then I talked this through with a good friend. She felt that it was an almost immediate answer to my prayer and encouraged me to go for it. This was no small dollar amount, so hence the bit of agonizing I was going through.

That's when God reminded me – as he did this summer – that this ministry is what he has for me at this stage of my life and that I need to take it seriously. I had once again fallen back into a waiting game to see what God would bring to me. He wanted me to take action. And so I did. I signed up for the classes and can't wait to delve into all that I will learn through this training.

I might not be back at the top of the roller coaster, but I have learned (again!) that God faithfully walks with me through the valleys and brings blessings that lift me out of them when I need them most.

Thanks for hanging on for the ride! If you're on your own ride right now, just remember who's at the controls.

"I know how to be brought low, and I know how to abound. In any and every circumstance,

I have learned the secret of facing plenty and hunger, abundance and need.

"I can do all things through him who strengthens me."
–Philippians 4:12-13

I don't want to leave you exhausted from that roller coaster ride, so let's look at a couple of blog posts that give us a much brighter and more hopeful outlook. They are both related to seasons which is the perfect analogy for how this life looks as we pass through good times and bad – just like God's creation.

"The Hope of Spring ... and More"

Day 527

My most recent posts on this site and on my ministry site have been a bit dark lately. And while it is important to be honest and transparent about this whole ugly grieving thing, I wanted to find a more hopeful "bent" for this next post.

Let's face it – this was an awful winter for so many of us, no matter where we live. Here in the Midwest, we were enticed into a hopeful expectation of a mild winter with our uneventful November and December. And then, *wham*! The rest of the winter was just so full of record lows, record low highs, record monthly snowfall, record days without sunshine and probably a lot of other nasty records that I can't recall.

That is hard on even the most Pollyanna-ish of us all.

For me, I also struggled with the second winter season without snow blowing equipment that worked. So, lots of hand shoveling – at one point with a broken shovel because I couldn't find any new ones in Des Moines. More than one "melt-down" out on my driveway ...

Add to that the difficulty of second-year widowhood and it resulted in the worst winter of my life.

"Gee, Lynne, if this is your idea of a more hopeful blog post, you might need to work on your approach a bit."

Admit it – you were thinking that, right? Don't worry, it's coming!

The past few days here in central Iowa have finally brought us a taste of what we hope lies ahead. Spring weather! I just finished walking my dog, Miss Daisy, and I was so encouraged by the sunshine, the kids out playing in the yards or riding their bikes, lots of dogwalkers, people in cars with their windows down, birds singing, a few brave flowers peeking out. That's a decent list, isn't it?

And it absolutely lifted my spirit out of that dark winter hole. I hope you've all been able to experience that as well. To me, that's part of what this spring season is about. New growth, new life, new hope, new season.

Because my brain is almost always in "blog mode," I look for lessons in the simplicity of life. One of the lessons learned as we get ready to turn the calendar to April is that, eventually, the winter ends. Oh sure, I know we could get a bit more snow, but we know it won't last.

We don't hope *in vain* for spring to arrive. God will undeniably usher it into our lives soon. And spring arrival is such a perfect example of how God ushers comfort, peace, healing, relief, and reprieve into our lives after a winter season in our soul.

I'm not saying God will always eliminate our heartaches. I know from personal experience that he does not. But I do believe he understands our limits and brings relief when we need it most.

Dale and I experienced an extremely difficult 2013. He suffered through one illness after another after another. So many trips to the ER and to hospitals across the state – with the associated bureaucratic headaches. I struggled to juggle work and household responsibilities with all the time and energy expended on his health needs. Add to that a couple of deaths in our family and we were both at the end of our ropes.

And then ... the calm. I kept waiting for another shoe to drop, but it did not. You might expect me to have learned a deep, theological lesson from that horrible year. *This* was my lesson – eventually it all came to an end.

Yep, that's all I got. I was a bit disappointed that it wasn't more profound. But then I realized that it was! God *does* bring our difficult seasons to an end. Maybe the difficulty is removed or resolved.

But maybe, the relief comes in the form of a new perspective. Maybe a scripture text, or a devotional, or a sermon, or a kind friend's words have caused you to see even your most difficult season a little differently.

Ultimately, the best way for us to view our difficulties is in light of eternity. If you're a believer, your hope lies not in the arrival of spring, but in the promise of heaven where there is no more pain, suffering, or tears. Where we reunite *forever* with our Savior – and with the loved ones we so long to see. I can't imagine a hope more glorious than that!

"May the God of hope fill you with all joy and peace in believing,so that by the power of the Holy Spirit you may abound in hope."
–Romans 15:13

"Seasonal Lessons"

Day 579

I've written a couple of blog posts that circled around this topic – one on this personal site and one on the ministry site, but neither one fully addressed my thoughts on this subject.

Maybe I just want to write on this topic because we've experienced about a 50-degree temperature change in the past few days! Let's hope there's a bit more depth to it than that ...

Lately, I'm hearing more and more people talk about how life is full of seasons. I've been saying that myself for the past 10 years or so. If you're one of my younger readers, say under 40, you may not have looked at life this way yet.

But for those of us who are likely in the last half of our earthly lives, this becomes more and more evident. And the more I thought about it, the more I saw parallels to the real weather seasons we experience.

When I was younger and I saw my life as overwhelmingly blessed, I just assumed that's how life should be. I certainly didn't think of it as just a "season" of my life. Why would I want this beautiful summer to turn into winter?

But eventually, as I experienced difficult times in my life, I started to see those parallels. Here are some of the life lessons I now see through this "seasonal lens."

- **Seasons are inevitable**. Just as surely as the snow melts and the tulips pop through, so will we experience times of joy and times of heartache, eventually. I now look at both of those times as seasons. It isn't just the difficult days that I equate to a winter season – it's everything. We move from one to another, and maybe back and forth.
- **Seasons come to an end**. Unless you live in some tropical paradise ... But here in the Midwest, we can be assured that we will not be buried in snow come August. And chances are high it won't hit 95 degrees in mid-January. Just as we all have our favorite weather season we hate to see come to an end, so will we want our good times to be endless. And conversely,

the winter seasons of our life do mercifully eventually come to an end and we see that hope of spring I wrote about earlier.

- **We don't know how long each season will last.** Every year is a bit different. When we lived in Stillwater, MN, we had a *three-foot* blizzard on Halloween! That's right! Go figure. Think that made for an excruciatingly long winter? Absolutely! But when we built our last home in 2000 here in Iowa, we had 80-degree days in December which made for a much shorter winter season. And a great year to be building a new home! Despite *The Farmer's Almanac* predictions, no one nails it 100%. Similarly, with your life seasons, seldom do you know how long either the good or the difficult times will last. (But God does.)

- **Some "mini-seasons" are just cold fronts or heat waves.** Within the four major seasons, we often find strange phenomenon showing up such as unexpected freezes or heat waves. They may be in and out in a couple of days, and then you return to what you expect of the season. Sure, they break it up a bit, for better or for worse, but there's usually not a long-lasting effect. When you go through a few days or weeks of "the blues," you might just be experiencing one of those cold fronts. Hopefully, your life returns to a sense of normalcy soon. And getting some joyful news in the middle of a tough year might just be a little heat respite for your winter-weary soul.

- **God knows every detail of the seasons.** Just as God is the author and creator of every season in every location from the beginning of time, so he also knows *exactly* what he's doing as he takes you through the seasons of your life. Nothing is arbitrary. No pain is wasted. Every one of your days is planned.

- **Look for the beauty in each season**. Of course, we all have our favorites. I toggle back and forth between spring and fall being my favorites. I love the new life that spring brings each year, but I also marvel at the spectacular colors of the fall. And even if we aren't fans of the extremes of summer and winter, I'm sure we have all admired some incredible beauty during those days.

What about the seasons of my life? Do I see beauty in each of them? Do you? Do I appreciate my favorite life season while I'm in it? Am I purposeful about finding the good in my difficult days? It's hard sometimes to do either, isn't it? It's so easy to take for granted our happy days – until they're taken from us and we're plunged into a harsh winter season. And then it's difficult to see how any good could come from it.

But trust God to be in each of them with you, even if you don't sense his presence. And know that he will never leave you in your dark days longer than necessary for him to teach you important life lessons, like entrusting these days to him.

"To everything there is a season, and a time to every purpose under the heaven ..."
Ecclesiastes 3:1 KJV

I tried extra hard to make sure my posts weren't always all about sadness and grieving. My goal was and still is to insert the joyful side of this season as well. And once in a great while, I wrote a post whose intention was to be a bit humorous. Not sure if I achieved that here but since I was the subject of this post, I found it refreshing to laugh at myself.

"Things That Are Hard to Do Alone"

Day 598

This past weekend, I got extra ambitious and decided to spray my mattress with a bottle promising to kill all the dust mites that have been eating my eyelashes for a while now. And along with that four-hour soaking project, I also decided to flip the queen-sized mattress, like any responsible mattress owner.

I have done it a few times over the last year or two, but it's always exhausting. On Saturday, as I was wrestling with this monstrosity, it "flipped out" and knocked my bedroom TV over, hitting the screen on the edge of the TV stand.

At first glance, it looked okay. But that night, as I was attempting to watch a little TV before dozing off, the screen looked like a bad imitation of a Picasso painting. Yep, gonna need a new TV ...

As I was contemplating the difficulty of this job, I was reminded again of how some things are hard, or even impossible, to do alone. Aha! There's a blog post topic for me! (I'm always sniffing one of those out ...)

And since I spend most of my time alone, especially here at home, I figured it was the perfect subject matter, and I should be able to have lots of ideas.

My goal was to have a humorous post for a change to balance out some of those pathetic ones I write from time to time. Because the mattress/TV thing is kind of funny, right?

So, I sat down at the computer – prayed like you know I do – and then could only think of *sad* things to do alone. That's *not* what I was looking for!

But in the spirit of full disclosure, I'm going to throw out a few sad things to do alone before continuing this quest.

- Go to a movie or a restaurant
- Go to a wedding or funeral
- Go anywhere
- Have a non-canine/feline conversation
- Cry on someone's shoulder
- Get or give a hug
- Put up Christmas lights

You get the idea. Yes, there are many things that are hard to do alone. That's all the space I'm allotting for sad things.

Back to my humor quest – I turned to my best friend, Google, and entered "Things that are hard to do alone." Surely Google had some ideas for me. Well, I was sent to a blog post from a woman in Oregon, also a widow some years back, who had written on this very subject.

It was hilarious!! I honestly laughed out loud reading it. So, I sent her an email, letting her know how much I enjoyed it and how I was writing on that exact same subject. Long story short – we are now Facebook friends.

As much as I was tempted to plagiarize some of her ideas (and she would likely have been okay with that), I'm committed to mostly original ideas here.

So, here is my list of "not sad" things that are hard or impossible to do alone.

- Flip a queen-sized mattress without destroying any other furniture ... or my back

- Drop myself off at the front door of anyplace in the rain
- Play Gin Rummy
- Make a toast to someone's health
- Ride a motorcycle without being the driver
- Win or lose an argument
- Blame anyone else when you lose things
- Play tennis or racquet ball
- Get the cat in the kennel

Now let's do some audience participation. I'd *love* to hear from any of my readers the *funny* things that are hard to do alone. And please, keep it G-rated. I have the power to delete your comment ...

"Then the Lord God said, 'It is not good that the man should be alone; I will make him a helper fit for him.'"
–Genesis 2:18

As you've likely ascertained, stepping back into the world is not a one-and-done kind of deal. It is a long-term adjustment to a loss that turns your world upside down. To some degree, you are never all the way back into the world, because that world doesn't exist anymore. But with God's grace and patient sanctification, you can redefine how your new world looks.

And so "the honest griever" steps into her new reality.

5

Memories and Regrets

Doesn't this chapter sound like a barrel of laughs? Memories during this season are the definition of "bittersweet." And there's very little that's bright and cheery about regrets. But, if I genuinely want to be "the honest griever," this chapter clearly needs to be included.

In my experience, memories and regrets overwhelmed me from the beginning of my grief journey and continue to this day. They are likely a constant companion to anyone who is grieving the loss of a long-term relationship.

Regrets Are Inevitable

Let's talk about regrets first. I think it's safe to say we all have them. I did. You can't be in a 35-plus-year relationship with someone without them. Let's face it, we are a sinful people! So, that sin will creep into any relationship, but especially that of husband and wife. I couldn't help but think of all the things I wish I had done differently throughout our lives together.

What regrets do you find yourself living with? Perhaps even some that aren't related to the death of a loved one. Regrets are pervasive in our lives, because there's so much that we don't do right! If you can make amends with the person you have offended, please do so! It will lift a huge burden off your heart.

If that relationship is irreversibly damaged, or the loved one has died, it gets more complicated. So what if you didn't have the opportunity to ask your loved one to forgive you for … anything? You know who loves to forgive? God. He will forgive you if you ask him. And there is nothing to be gained by living out your regrets again and again. Learn from them? Of course. But don't camp out there. Rest in God's forgiveness and let that be enough.

Embrace Your Memories

As I looked through the posts I wanted to include in this section, I found it interesting that all four were written within five months of each other, and within the first year after Dale's death. Obviously, the whole issue of memories and regrets was front and center in those early days of grieving.

But here's the thing. I'm at the two-and-a-half-year mark as I write this, and I'm *still* bombarded with memories that can either bring a smile to my heart, or bring me to my knees in tears. They haven't significantly slowed down. But I guess the fact that I stopped writing about them means they have become part of the landscape of my widowhood. I expect them to be a large part of my life, so the experience is not making it into the blog pages anymore. It's one example of how the grief we live with eventually changes our lives permanently and molds us into a new person.

So now let's look at some of the posts that addressed this all-encompassing world of memories.

This first post is one of many times that music grabbed me by the heart. This one caused me to ask the question the song writer poses.

"Five More Minutes"

Day 148

With apologies to my non-country-music-lover readers, I'm going to use the theme for this post from a recent #1 hit on the country charts by Scotty McCreery entitled, you guessed it, "Five More Minutes." I first heard this song a month or two ago and without even listening to the verses, I knew that there was a message here, not just for me, but hopefully for many of you.

Before I get to the heart stab I felt upon hearing it, I'll give you a brief synopsis of the song – and a little country music writing tutorial for you country-music illiterates! Often the song writer will tell a story with each verse, using the chorus as the tie that binds. In this case, the verses talk about children wanting to play a little longer, a young couple wanting their goodnight kiss on the porch to last longer, the high school senior football player wanting just a few more minutes on that football field – and then finally, the writer asking for more time with his dying grandfather.

But when I heard the song the first time, I only paid attention to the chorus and I immediately asked myself this question, "What would I say to Dale if I could have him back for just five more minutes?" (Although I would seriously never ask him to leave the glory of heaven to come back to earth for even that short period of time!) Would there be enough time to make up for the things I didn't say before he died? And surprisingly, I decided that yes, I could say a *lot* in five minutes.

We were blessed that, in the ten months Dale spent in the assisted living facility, God brought restoration to our marriage after some very difficult years dealing with his dementia. I was able to go from being his full-time caregiver to his wife again. So, we did have time to reminisce about the many good years we had together and thank God for the blessings throughout those years.

I was able to ask Dale to forgive me for the times I hadn't been as patient as I should have been, to which he replied, "I already have." What an incredible gift that was to me at a vulnerable time. It speaks volumes about the kind of person Dale was. Kind and loving and *forgiving* to the end.

And yet, I felt so strongly about the message in this title that I did stop and honestly address the question. What would I say if I had five more minutes? I would be much more intentional about letting him know how much I loved him and how much his unconditional love meant to me for over 35 years. I would thank him for his faithfulness to me, for his great sense of humor, for his outlook on life, for his patience, kindness and understanding, and for his quiet faith.

I would also be more intentional about asking for his forgiveness for all the times I fell short of being the wife that I knew God wanted me to be. And maybe I'd even ask forgiveness for the times I felt compelled to correct the spelling in his grocery lists! Or not ...

While my message from this song was about doing something completely impossible – bringing Dale back for five minutes – its original intent was, in part, to challenge the listener to consider how we would treat five more minutes with a loved one.

What would *you* do with those five minutes? What would be the most important message? And who comes to mind when you ponder the question? Just what are the scenarios that pop into your mind? What about sending a child off to college? Or seeing a friend move across the country? Or thanking a favorite teacher or boss? Or just seeing your spouse or child walk out the door to work or school in the morning? Simple, everyday interactions in which those five minutes would become very precious to you.

So, this post is really food for thought. Who are the people in your life who need you to fill up five minutes with words of encouragement, or repentance, or love? We all have them – lots of them, most likely. Let me encourage you to take that little snippet of time and use it for the good of others – and you'll find that you're blessed in the process. I know it's good advice for me as well.

And it's not just good inter-personal relationship advice, it's also biblical. "Let no corrupting talk come out of your mouths, but only such as is good for building up, as fits the occasion, that it may give grace to those who hear" (Ephesians 4:29).

May God give you and me the courage, the heart, and the opportunities to use our five minutes well!

I share a perspective in this next post that, frankly, caught me a bit by surprise. Maybe you, too, will find it unique and hopefully applicable to your life regardless of what you're experiencing in this moment.

"The Good Ol' Days"

Day 235

People often joke that the only thing good about the good ol' days is that they're gone. While there is some truth to that, I still believe we all can look back at times in our lives when happy and pleasant memories bring a smile to our hearts and fill us with the warmth of nostalgia.

As I continue grieving the loss of Dale, I am spending a fair amount of time reminiscing about our "good ol' days" together. It's one of the ways I can stay connected to him and focus on times that make me grateful for the life we had together. But, it's bittersweet. As great as those times were, they are gone, never to return – and that also brings me sorrow.

Even during the days as Dale's physical and mental health were deteriorating, I tried to maintain an attitude of being grateful for what we had and not being sad that it was over. Easier said than done, for sure, and there were many days when I failed. Can I apply that state of mind to my current situation?

As I look through pictures, or just linger over some heart-warming memories, I regret that I didn't cherish those times as much as I should have while they were happening. Can you relate to that? Don't we all do that to a certain degree? We don't appreciate what we have until it's gone.

I suppose that's part of our human nature to have a greater appreciation in retrospect. And there is likely some truth to the idea that we tend to remember what was good about those days and either forget or bury what might not have been so great. But I do believe happy memories are a comforting gift during dark days.

Recently, a challenging thought came to me – "Am I appreciating *these* good ol' days like I should?" That's a pretty crazy question, isn't it? Really? I should be appreciating the days where I'm grieving the worst loss of my life? How is that even applicable here? And yet, somehow, I felt that it was.

I just finished some more "light bedtime reading" in Randy Alcorn's (nearly 500-page) book entitled *If God is Good – Faith in the Midst of Suffering and Evil* (Multnomah, 2014). I'm sure some of you are thinking, "Seriously, Lynne, can't you find something more 'Disney-esque' to read?"

I wrote in an earlier post about how God does his best work in our lives through our trials, and that was definitely one of the main themes in the book. The author cited story after heartbreaking story of people and couples and families who had been through tremendous difficulties in their lives (or were still in them) – and were often very angry with God or whomever they could blame for the tragedy at the time.

And yet, in retrospect, many of these stories ended with those involved being grateful for the lessons they learned, for the deepening of their faith, for the way they saw God using their tragedy to help others. They would even go so far as to say that, despite the horrific experience they went through, they wouldn't trade it for all they gained in their knowledge and relationship with God because of it.

These are powerful testimonies. It's almost hard to believe – that someone would be so grateful for the worst days of their lives. And yet, we must take them at their word and learn from what they share with us.

So, will I look back on this season of my life and be grateful for it? How about appreciating the good ol' days *right now*? Mind you, I do clearly see God working in my life and am grateful for the lessons learned since Dale's death. But, if I'm honest, I'd have to say that I sometimes come to that gratitude a bit reluctantly.

I would still *much* rather not be going through this pain, even if the outcome is for my good. That's my "human-ness" speaking. Deep in my soul, I know that's not where it should end. Paul says in his letter to the Romans, "... we rejoice in our sufferings, knowing that suffering produces endurance, and endurance produces character, and character produces hope, and hope does not put us to shame, because God's love has been poured into our hearts through the Holy Spirit who has been given to us." That's a beautiful promise!

So, my prayer for myself and for all of you is that we will be able to live more "in the moment," regardless of whether we are in sunshine or storms, and that our hearts would be open to, and even searching for, the lessons we can learn regardless of the forecast.

One of the phenomena surrounding memories is how they can sneak up on you when you least expect it – and come from the most unlikely sources. Not only is that true of memories, it's true of grief in general. We can anticipate some events that will bring us to tears. But so often, we are blindsided by them. Read on!

"Kitchen Spring Cleaning Tears"

Day 261

Is it just me, or did we completely miss spring this year? That might explain why I'm doing my spring housecleaning in July! Not that it's spring-like weather now either. Maybe next year.

But this has been on my master "to do" list for some time now so I decided to get started. I do the easier rooms first (I know, that's not what the experts recommend) like the spare bedroom, bath, etc. My office is always a bit challenging because it becomes a catch-all for things that I don't know where to store permanently. I tackled that room last week and it was as tedious as I feared.

I was also somewhat prepared to run into items that would bring back memories. Specifically, I had saved so many birthday, anniversary, and Christmas cards that Dale had given me through the years, and I found myself reading and crying through all of them. Such a sweet reminder of the love we shared for all those years. But bittersweet all the same. It was an exhausting room!

I took a few days off before tackling one of the biggest sub-projects of them all – the *kitchen*! I take everything out of every drawer, every shelf, every cubby hole and clean them all. It entails checking expiration dates, purging my two junk drawers, deep cleaning appliances and blinds, and other miscellaneous monotonous tasks. It's a full day commitment, however you slice it.

I was prepared for all of that. What I wasn't prepared for was the barrage of memories and tears from the kitchen items!

- The half-packet of chili seasoning that I used for Dale's chili recipe. He had just "winged it" in the past, but it was so good that eventually he taught me how to make it – and I even passed the recipe along to my mom. And yes, part of the recipe was a half packet of seasoning.
- The popcorn pan and bowls and popcorn and oil. He made the *best* popcorn the old-fashioned way – on the stove top with lots of butter. Popcorn and a movie at home were always a treat.
- Pink sugar packets for his coffee. Whenever we'd eat out and he'd have coffee after dinner, he'd always ask the waitress for "the little pinkies."
- Coffee mug from his mission trip to Brazil. It had the first verse of Psalm 23 inscribed on it in Portuguese and Dale used to store his toothbrush in it. Apparently, I decided it belonged with the rest of the coffee mugs after he passed.
- Tupperware gravy shaker. Dale was the expert in this area – I just bought the packets if I was making gravy! But I have many memories of holiday meals where Dale oversaw the gravy-making, and faithfully combined milk, flour and seasonings to make a delicious, lump-free gravy!

I know there is a special camaraderie that comes from sharing a meal with someone. So, after 30-some years of eating together, I shouldn't be surprised at the depth of emotions that these everyday items elicited from me. So, I had a good cleansing cry during one of my biggest cleansing projects …

After pulling myself together, I took on the only part of the cupboards left – the pantry! Another place that tends to expand its contents miraculously, it seems. Dale moved to his assisted living facility in December 2016, so a full 19 months have passed since we regularly ate together. Add to that the fact that I've pretty much quit eating processed foods.

So, not unexpectedly, there were a lot of items to be tossed. Foods that Dale used to eat that I didn't like, items that I wasn't going to indulge in anymore, and *many* expired boxes and cans. Talk about a purging! Not counting some baking products, the only food items left when I finished were a jar of peanut butter, a jar of strawberry jam, some crackers, a bag of popcorn and one can of dog food (I'll probably pass on that …)

Oh my goodness! I felt like Old Mother Hubbard! Seriously, it was just a bit surreal to think that there was really nothing of substance left in the pantry. It made me chuckle to myself and yet, at the same time, I felt a little melancholy. Like I had closed a door on that season of my life.

Was there a lesson in this for me? It was clearly an emotional process and I wondered just what God might be teaching me through this. I've often said that God doesn't waste any of our pain, so with this new onslaught of tearful memories, just what was his message here? Was it just another thing to grieve through? Or was there more to be gleaned?

I always feel like it's a new beginning when I've done some major cleaning out – whether it's clothes closets, junk drawers, or pantries. I start fresh with every intention of not letting things get out of hand this time.

As I approach the nine-month anniversary of Dale's death, is it time for a new beginning there, too? Honestly, I don't want a new beginning because I'm not even close to being done with this season of grieving. And I'm definitely not ready to let go of all the memories we shared. Ironically, I feel closest to Dale when I'm crying over a past memory, and I don't want to lose that.

But, there is something to be said for finding a new "normal." I can't dwell strictly in the past; my life going forward is one without Dale in it and that's my new reality. However, my future is one in which God is personally and faithfully and second-by-second deeply entrenched. And I couldn't be more grateful knowing that he goes with me each day, guiding me through this darkness and teaching me long-lasting life lessons. *That* is the only way I can find a new normal. Yes, it's without Dale, but my relationship with God is deeper than it's ever been. That's the trade-off. I must trust that I have the better deal now.

Let me be clear, looking for a new normal or a new beginning does not mean I'm moving on from my life with Dale. I am, however, trying to move forward. The memories that so often bring me to tears will continue to be part of my life, maybe forever.

Because, guess what? I kept the gravy shaker, the pink sugar packets, and his Brazilian coffee mug. Some memories just can't be purged.

"Fear not, for I am with you; be not dismayed, for I am your God;
I will strengthen you, I will help you, I will uphold you with my righteous right hand."
Isaiah 41:10

In this next post, I address something I struggled with for months after Dale's death. I found my memories primarily of our particularly good times. I wasn't spending time on anything that would make me sad and I often wondered if I was being dishonest with myself, sticking my head in the proverbial sand. How could I do that if I'm "the honest griever?" I come to terms with my approach to happy memories in this post.

"Memories through Rose-Colored Glasses?"

Day 306

I seemed to have entered a new phase or season in this grieving process, and I'm not necessarily a big fan of it. Every day, multiple times a day, the oddest thing will bring back a memory of my life with Dale. The frequency and the intensity are greater than in the months soon after his death. And it's not the items you would expect, like a past anniversary card, or his wallet, or other sentimental items.

Oh no, it's the TV commercial about metal paneling for your garage or out-building. Yep, that takes me immediately back to when we built our home and barn on our last acreage. And not just to the recollection of that event, but to the feelings and emotions that surrounded that time in our lives.

Or maybe it's the commercial for the Italian restaurant that sends me instantly back to Gino's Italian restaurant over on Sixth Avenue. That was "our place." I often called it our *Cheers*, because everyone knew our name. (Even the grandkids would invoke Grandpa's name to try and get an advantage on a busy night ...). It had been Dale's hangout since the '70s and it became ours as well. Every memory from our dinner dates there is a happy one. So, this TV commercial blindsided me when I least expected it.

And just so you don't think that all I do is watch TV commercials, I can be cooking something mundane in the kitchen and have the same phenomenon occur. It's not necessarily even a meal we had together often, but somehow, I'm still transported back to a happy time revolving around a similar meal.

Seeing happy couples anywhere; TV, movies, real life, also brings a little stab to my heart as I long for those days that we had. And don't even get me started on music! Always lots of emotions tied to those love songs.

Powerful, take-me-back-in-time emotions associated with all these memories.

In case you're wondering, it is always a happy memory and yet it almost always leads me to tears. I guess that would be the definition of "bittersweet." I'm so blessed to have had these happy times to miss, and yet there's also always a sadness knowing they are over.

There is a general phenomenon that I'd guess many of us have experienced in our lives where we mostly remember the good times in our past. I've always suspected that our minds were somehow shielding us from bad memories, times that we'd rather forget.

I wondered if there was any science behind this, so I went to my friend Google and, lo and behold, there was an article in the *Scientific American* (Bret Stetka, "How the Brain Purges Bad Memories, scientificamerican.com, July 31, 2015) that did in fact discuss the conclusion that there are some connections in our brain between a couple of key areas that can cause memory "extinction," particularly with unpleasant or fearful experiences. How about that! Enough science for now. Take it or leave it.

It might make sense to assign that phenomenon to what I'm going through right now – remembering and grieving over all the good times, as if that is all we ever had. And perhaps there is some truth to that.

But despite the science, I have a different theory. Simply put, I don't believe there's anything to grieve about the difficult times. Why would you long for and miss past difficulties? (This is different from having regrets over things in our past, which is a topic for another day!)

But there is *much* to grieve about the good times. And please don't misunderstand - Dale and I had both kinds throughout our 35-plus-year relationship. We lived in the real world where things like pride and stubbornness and self-centeredness and insecurities and impatience and health problems and dementia stole our joy on a regular basis. But is there really anything to grieve about those times? Do we miss that? I think not!

So, to officially bring the title topic of rose-colored glasses into the discussion, I would like to publicly declare that I am *not* viewing my past life with Dale through them. I am not sad that any of our sin-driven bad moments are over. I am only missing those moments where God showered blessings into our lives in big and small ways, literally for decades. For that I am eternally grateful, and for that, I am now grieving.

"And I will make them and the places all around my hill a blessing, and I will send down the showers in their season; they shall be showers of blessing."

Ezekiel 34:26

A few blog posts had virtually no deep, profound messages or lessons, such as this next one. But it does shine a light on my husband's character, and perhaps you will get a bit of a chuckle from the stories.

"A Heart Full of Messages"

Day 329

It's been clear from several of my past blog posts that I've been doing my spring house cleaning for the last few months. Yes, it's now become summer and fall cleaning, but, whatever.

The only area that's been left to tackle for the past month or so has been the master closet. But before you start to feel sad for me, I have already gone through all of Dale's clothes. In fact, he and I went through most of it together before he moved to the care facility.

And I go through my clothes on a regular basis, so this really wasn't a big job that I was dreading. I just hadn't gotten around to it yet.

One of the items on the very top shelf was the stuffed heart Dale received from the hospital staff after his triple bypass surgery nearly 15 years ago. Not only did it serve as the item he was to clutch if he needed to cough or sneeze, but it also became the place that staff, visitors, and friends added their words of wisdom for Dale during his stay.

I kept debating whether it was something to keep or not. I've read the messages many times over the past years, so there weren't any new revelations on it. But I did find myself smiling a lot as I did reread all of them today.

Then it hit me. This would make a great blog post! And not a sad one, for a change. The messages on it covered the full spectrum of what you might write to someone recovering from heart surgery. Especially someone like Dale whose circle of friends was so very wide and diverse.

But before I share all that was on it, I have two favorite memories from that experience that still make me smile today.

- Dale was so proud of this one and I share it with apologies to my readers (myself included) who aren't great fans of bathroom humor. For any of you who have experienced either your own surgery or that of a loved one, you know that there is one very important activity that must occur before you can go home. Or in this case, be moved out of CCU.

  That's right. It's the bathroom job. Once the spirit moved Dale, literally, it was a great day and a sign that he was healing. One problem – as he liked to tell it – he broke the toilet. Yep.

Had to get the top maintenance guys up there with their big snake to get things moving again. And even funnier (to me), was when he did get moved out of CCU, this story, and his reputation, had preceded him to the telemetry floor where he was moved. Everyone got such a kick out of this story, but no one more than Dale.

- The second incident happened while he was completely out of it, recovering in his room. He wanted me to take a picture of him right after surgery because he was curious about what he looked like. We even got clearance from the hospital staff to do it.

  But when the time came for the photo op, I freaked out a bit and couldn't do it. Keep in mind, he had not regained consciousness yet. I was accompanied into his room by both of his daughters, so one of them graciously offered to take the picture for me.

  This was before all the smartphone cameras, so her camera had a little flash on it. As soon as she snapped the picture with the flash, Dale's eyes flew wide open and we *all* completely freaked out. We ran out of his room, down a staircase for a few floors and ended up lost somewhere in the employee cafeteria! Only later did we find out from the nurse that he never really regained consciousness then; it was just the body's reaction to the flash. That one still makes me laugh to this day!

So, with that backdrop, here are the unaltered messages from his hospital "heart" – with no names attached!

"Hurry and get home. I love you!"

"Dale, be good."

"Faker! Get well soon! God bless ..." (Yes, that was all from one person!)

"Keep smiling."

"Best wishes for a speedy recovery from the bottom of my heart." (Strategically written at the bottom, of course!)

"I can do all things through Christ who strengthens me. Phil 4:13. We're praying for you!"

"Get well, I [heart] U"

"Get rolling soon"

"Good luck"

"Get well soon!"

"Love you, Dad, you're doing great!"

"We want you home – take care"

"Patients like you make everything worthwhile. You are great. Never forget your first Colgate shower."

" 'Bout time"

'You'll do anything to get out of vacuuming! I love you! Come home soon." (OK, that was me, signed Nurse Ratched – *One Flew Over the Cuckoo's Nest*)

"You're a good guy. I've enjoyed taking care of you. Stay healthy!"

"I'll send all the good plumbers your way. Beware of 'the stick lady!' Best of luck!" (editorial note – stick lady was the rehab person whom Dale wasn't really fond of ...)

"Hope you have a speedy recovery. You've been a great patient."

"Thanks for letting me take care of you. You were a joy!"

"Keep up the great work!"

Such a nice collection of sentiments, but a definite theme that he was a patient the staff all enjoyed caring for. Our main CCU nurse was pregnant with twins at the time and before we left her floor, Dale wanted me to give her some cash to use for any upcoming baby expenses. So much like him.

Nothing more to add. No deep lessons. Not even a scripture text this time! Hope you got a smile or a chuckle out of the stories or the messages. I'm smiling as I type this.

Memory Benefits

Before we leave this topic, I'd like to emphasize one point I briefly touched on in one of the posts. The fact that, despite the pain they can inflict, I'm not willing to give up these memories. First, they are single-handedly the best way for me to stay connected to Dale and the life we had. I feel closest to him when I'm reliving a happy memory.

Secondly, I do hope with time, they become less bitter and "more sweet." But regardless of where I am on that bittersweet spectrum, I know they are a gift from God and a reminder of past blessings he has bestowed on me.

I urge you to see your good memories in this light as well. May they warm your hearts and bring a smile to your faces during any of your difficult days.

And so "the honest griever" learns how to live with both memories and regrets.

6

Friendship

This is a chapter that will not have any associated blog posts to illustrate my points. That's because there are some hard truths and painful experiences to share and I haven't wanted to do that in a post that could ultimately be hurtful. But the "honest griever" must address it.

How Many Ways Can We Lose Friends?

This is such a *huge* issue for widows and widowers and others suffering through significant losses. What I've learned through my own painful experience and what I've heard from virtually every widow(er) I've talked with and countless more whose articles and blog posts I've read is this: When we lost our spouses, we lost friends.

Now mind you, the losses weren't for the same reasons across the board. But that doesn't mean there wasn't pain associated with most of the loss of friends. So, let's take a deeper look into how and why this happens.

One of the most common ways that friends are lost is when the friendship was part of a couples group. When all the socializing is done as husbands and wives, and suddenly you don't have that other half, it's hard! For *both* sides. Everyone is keenly aware that one of the pieces is missing and yet, I think it's common to try and pretend that the hole isn't that big. But to the one without the spouse, it's *huge*! Enter … awkwardness.

Sadly, the resolution to this awkwardness is often for the newly widowed person to step out, and take the elephant in the room with them. One possible compromise in a situation like this is for the men or women to continue getting together socially. But even with that solution, we usually know that the couples are still gathering, and that knowledge brings with it a longing to still be part of the group. There's no perfect solution when an even-numbered batch of friends becomes odd.

I guess in some ways I was fortunate I didn't lose "couple friends." Because Dale had been failing for several years, our couple friend outings had already come to an end. In many cases, I remained friends with the women in those groups.

In some cases, the loss of friends has a natural path that slowly but eventually ends up with both parties having little in common anymore. There's no defined moment when they decide to call it quits. The friendship just reaches a natural end. In some ways, it's no different than any friendship that diminishes over time as the individuals become different people and grow apart.

What I have noticed regarding the whole "nothing in common" phenomenon is that even though some friends are still interested in getting together with me, it seems they are most comfortable interacting with me as if I haven't been through this traumatic loss. If they never ask how I'm doing or want to discuss how my life is now different, then from my perspective the friendship has been altered significantly. And to a certain degree, it's less satisfying to me because I can't truly be myself. I'm pretending that nothing has changed, when in some ways, everything has changed. And so has this friendship.

Now, let's tackle the most difficult way to lose friendships. It's what I experienced in the weeks and months after Dale died. Many friends were uncomfortable around me. They didn't know what to do with me. It was easier to pretend that the death of my husband wasn't the devastation that it was to me.

And on the flip side, I didn't know how to deal with that distance and that denial from friends. It was one of the most painful things I experienced after Dale's death. When I needed them most, I lost friends. I shed many tears over this at a time when I didn't need more heartache.

When I was in the early stages of this heartbreaking loss, I *so* needed people to be present in my life. To acknowledge how much pain I was in. To sit and cry with me. To check in regularly. To let me process this loss. To share all that this wonderful man meant to me.

And make no mistake, I *did* have friends who did all the above. And to this day, I'm deeply grateful for their kindnesses. Why wasn't that enough? Why did I need all my friends to be there for me? I don't have any good answers for that. Was it pride? Was it a feeble attempt to fill this huge hole in my life with friends' compassion? Was it a way to keep the full weight of the pain at bay? Maybe some of each. Honestly, there was very little thinking or reasoning with it. It was all emotions. It's just how I felt and there was little I could do to change that.

Regardless of the reasons for the breakdown of some friendships, it was painful and added to the weight on my heart.

Repair Is Possible

Here's one "rabbit-trail" piece of advice I'd like to pass along to you readers on *both* sides of this situation. If you haven't been the friend you wanted to be through their painful loss, I highly encourage you to step back in. How does that work? Apologize sincerely for not being there. Don't load up on excuses. "I've been kind of busy ..." Just say you're sorry and express your desire to step back into their world and be the supporter and comforter they likely still need. And then do it!

For those of you who are the grievers, and likely hurt by someone in this season, open your heart. Acknowledge how difficult it must be for your friend to come to you with "hat in hand," so to speak. Simply put ... forgive them. Don't you want them back in your life? Couldn't you use another friend who is now desiring a deeper relationship with you?

If the offending friend steps back in with a sincere apology, and the griever graciously accepts that apology and forgives, it is the definition of WIN-WIN!

Blessings through the Loss

So, back to our main path. Let's take a more positive turn. What are the silver linings through this heartache? That's an easy question for me to answer. My biggest silver lining was the ministry. Without those hurtful experiences, I would not have been equipped to begin the ministry that God so clearly called me to. How could I teach people the importance of "being a blessing to your grieving friend" if I hadn't experienced the pain of that loss?

As is so often the case with God, he uses our pain and heartache for eventual good. And there has been *much* good that has come from this. The ministry and all that comes with that has become the essence of my life in this season. I've never felt more called to anything in my life. I have more passion for this ministry than any job I've held in a nearly 25-year corporate career.

God has reminded me that, I too, have stepped away from friends during their darkest hours. I've not known what to say, and consequently said nothing. I've made wrong assumptions, which ultimately added more pain to my friends' lives. I wish I knew who all I have offended in the past so I could specifically apologize to them. The best I can do is be the right kind of friend now and teach others how to do that as well.

God has also helped me let go of any anger or bitterness resulting from these situations. I'll never forget that day when God essentially spoke to me (no, not out loud, but in my soul) and said, "If you don't let go of any anger or bitterness, you will limit what I want to do through this ministry." Yikes! Who wants to get in God's way?? Not me, so that day was one of many turning points as I began to shed the hurt and replace it with purpose.

The transformation in my soul was life-changing. I couldn't be more grateful for God's patience and grace as I slowly, but eventually, landed in the place where God could use me in a powerful way.

Do you struggle with hurts that were inflicted by friends, perhaps unintentionally, but are still deeply painful? How can you find purpose in that pain? Maybe it shines a light on your own shortcomings in the past, as it did with me. Perhaps it gives you a more compassionate heart as you walk along *your* friends who are grieving. Maybe it's even a necessary purging of friendship where God is showing you who you can count on for the long haul. Be open to how God wants to use this pain for good in your life.

"Area of Friendship"

I also want to share with you the way I view the changes to my friendship landscape. I call it my "Area of Friendship." And yes, it is the mathematical calculation of "area." My apologies to those of you who have math anxiety, but I'm hopeful that the concept is clear enough that you'll be blessed by the application.

To refresh everyone, the way to calculate the area of a rectangle is to multiply the length by the width. So, if a rectangle measures 6 feet by 8 feet, the area is 48 feet. Everyone still with me? Great.

Now let's assume a few things as we apply this to the "Area of Friendship." But instead of assigning actual numbers to the length and width, I want to just assign categories. Stay with me!

This first rectangle represents my "Area of Friendship" *before* Dale's death. The length (long side) represents the number of friends I had at that point. The width (short side) represents the "average" depth of those friendships. Hence length times width equals the "Area of Friendship." Can you get your head around that concept?

Number of Friends

Average Depth of Friendships

Even though there are no numbers, hopefully you can visually grasp that we've theoretically quantified the totality of my friendships.

Enter Dale's death and associated aftermath. What does the "Area of Friendship" look like now?

Number of Friends

Average Depth of Friendships

Do you see what happened here? The number of friends I have now may be less than before Dale's death, but the *depth* of those friendships has increased significantly. The friends who have stuck with me through this season, and the new friends I've developed *because* of Dale's death, contribute to the deeper and more satisfying friendships that I now enjoy.

I wouldn't even be surprised if my "Area of Friendship" is actually larger *now* than it was before Dale died. What if you did the same analysis on your friendships. Would you see a similar pattern? Isn't it just like God to, not only bless us with those deeper relationships, but to help us recognize it?

So, this is the positive note I want to end on for this uncomfortable chapter. Regardless of how or why our friendships have changed, the result is that God can bring *much* good out of that journey. My heart is full of gratitude. May God help us all to always see what we've gained and not what we've lost.

And so "the honest griever" learns to celebrate her new "area of friendship."

7

Milestones

It's funny how a major loss can often cause us to look at our life in two sections – before and after the event. That's why so much of the timing in my life is viewed through the lens of the anniversary of Dale's death. The other powerful milestone is our wedding day, the *other* end of the emotional spectrum.

Your milestones will vary depending on what loss you're struggling with. Of course the milestone could be marking a death, but divorces, cancer diagnoses, job losses, disabilities, or any number of other life-altering events also come with their own set of difficult dates.

Death Anniversaries

It should come as no surprise that we mark off all the days that remind us of this loss. In the early days after Dale died, every Monday was an anniversary of sorts. A milestone that ticked off the time that was passing, even though I felt that my life had come to a screeching halt.

Before long, I found myself looking at the sixteenth of every month as the milestone in place of the Mondays. Then that morphed into six-month intervals and now I've reached the point where the only date that gets my attention in any significant way is October 16.

I'm sure you've all heard or experienced the concept of the first year of firsts. The hope, and to a certain degree, expectation, is that once we've survived the first birthday, Father's Day, wedding day, Easter, Thanksgiving, Christmas, etc., etc., without them, we are now cleared for the good life. I wish it were that simple. I'll talk about this in more detail in later chapters, but suffice it to say, one year doesn't heal all wounds.

In addition to the death anniversary, all those special days I just listed and many more can cause anxiety. It can be a virtual landmine! Every time you turn around, there's another date that brings back memories. Most of the time we walk through these dates with few people aware of the sadness they elicit, as it should be. We can't openly grieve through every day that brings a little stab to our hearts.

But it should serve as a reminder for all of us to be kind to those whose paths we cross every day, especially if that person is a tad grumpy! We never know what they're struggling with, or if *this day* is a difficult anniversary for them. Chances are high that everyone you meet is dealing with something. Widows and widowers do not have the market on difficult days!

Places we went with our loved one can also bring back powerful emotions, and like grief, can sneak up on us when we least expect it. Honestly, I don't think there's much we can do about them, except try to embrace any warm, happy memories they bring back to you. And move on quickly if the heartache is too overwhelming.

Because the milestone days were such a big part of the journey, I want to share my blog posts as I passed through those significant dates. Interestingly, I had to go to the ministry blog posts (not the personal ones I'm using here) to retrieve the two-year anniversary post. My goal at that point was primarily education and enlightenment, not grief processing.

I'll share the death anniversary posts back to back to see what changed, and what remained the same. Word of warning, some of these may be hard to read. Buckle up!

"Reflections on the Six-Month Anniversary"

Day 182

How in the world have I been without Dale for six months already, as of today? That was one of my first thoughts as I started writing this post. I think it's similar to what they say about raising children – the days are long, but the years are short. In my case, the days (and evenings) are long and the months are short.

I've been "chewing" on this topic for a while now, knowing that I wanted to share at some point what I'm learning personally through this journey. And I anticipated that it would have a similar structure to an earlier post, "What Your Grieving Friend Wants You to Know."

It would have nice defined bullet points and I might even come up with another Top-Ten-type list.

And yet, despite all the many dog walks where I've worked on this topic, for the longest time it just seemed like everything was all muddled up and interwoven and random – kind of like a batch of spaghetti. So, I was seriously concerned that nothing was going to fall into place.

About a week ago, the simplest of messages landed in my soul. The defining truth on which I hang everything is this: **God is all-sufficient**! It's his sovereignty, his direction, his Holy Spirit guiding and teaching me truths that I never would have known had I not entered this dark place. He wants me to not only know, but to experience what it means for him to be my all-sufficiency. God is my *everything* through this journey. I must accept that everything and everyone could fall away, but his Word and his presence never will. And that must be enough.

So, with that backdrop and that filter on my reflections, here are some nitty-gritty lessons and revelations that have come to me over these last difficult months. Hang in there with me! The ride starts out a little bumpy ...

Let me get the most painful revelations out of the way first. Losing Dale is the single most difficult, heart-breaking experience of my life. Not a day goes by that I don't miss him terribly and shed tears over all that we'll never have again on this earth. The pain should not be surprising. A marriage is a covenant relationship and when one of the partners is taken away, it's like having half of your body ripped apart because we become one flesh.

It's a double-edged sword; God had a perfect and precious design for marriage, and I was blessed by that, but sin entered the world in the Garden of Eden and his beautiful creation and plan has been tainted ever since. So, the sharp side of that sword is the pain that comes with the loss. But it helps me understand why this is a loss like no other I've ever experienced.

And don't think you can get through this without much shedding of tears. It's part of grieving and how God made us. The Bible is chock full of examples of people going through hard times with many tears. Jesus himself, wept at the death of Lazarus. It's natural, it's necessary, and it's divinely ordained. Check out the Psalms sometime for proof of this!

When people ask me if I have good days and bad days, I must honestly respond that every day has pain and sadness in it. *And* every day has blessing in it. It's just a matter of degree. Some days the grief and loneliness are overwhelming and come in waves of tears and heartache. Other days can feel much more normal with people and activities that are blessings to me and make me smile or laugh. It's like a sliding scale from 1 to 100 and I glide back and forth between both ends of the grief scale. So, every day is a mixture. The key is to be grateful for, and watchful for, the good things.

Stay with me for one other painful revelation I've learned and then I promise there will be light at the end of this blog tunnel! The other stark reality is that this is barely the beginning of a long, arduous journey. Virtually every widow I've talked with or whose words I've read candidly shares that healing never completely comes, and it often takes many years to even come out of the fog. Honestly, it's not very encouraging and I'd prefer to ignore their hard-earned wisdom! It's much more a process of learning how to live with the hole in your life and focusing on what God wants to do with the new creature that we've become. I trust that not an ounce of my pain is wasted. God has plans for it and I can't wait to be part of that.

So, let's turn a corner and see how and where joy can still make a home in this life I'm now living.

First and foremost, I'm discovering amazing new truths about God's character and his ways that resonate deep in my soul *because* I'm grieving. I'm afraid I won't be able to do justice to this phenomenon with my mere words. But it's becoming so clear to me that God does some of his greatest, most permanent work in our lives when we're going through trials. At the core, it can be as simple as, "How could I see the light if I wasn't in the darkness?"

How much more clearly do I see God and his love for me once all the peripheral "clutter" of life is stripped away? How could I so look forward to an eternity with Christ and no more suffering if I hadn't suffered here on earth? How could I clearly hear God's voice if I weren't forced to sit quietly and listen for it? How would I know if my God-given faith could stand this test if I wasn't asked to trust it alone? I could go on and on, but I hope you get the picture. This season will be one of incredible growth if I trust the one whose hand I am in.

God's Word is full of people going through trials and struggles and pain and tears because it is through those times that God moved mightily in their lives. He uses those experiences to deepen our love for him and to allow him to use us to reach out to others by sharing what we've learned.

I have found it to be extremely comforting to focus on reading scripture, devotionals, and books that will speak to this season of my life, written by people I trust and whose theology is solid. A great devotional I'm reading is entitled *Streams in the Desert* (Zondervan, rev. 1999) and a very insightful book I just finished is Timothy Keller's *Walking with God through Pain and Suffering* (Penguin Books, 2015). How's that for a little light reading before bed? Both are excellent at shining light on the many ways God clearly wants to use our tough times for his good.

Does God understand our pain? Count on it! He sent his only Son, Jesus, to *truly* suffer and die on our behalf. That pain was turned into incredible joy as we just celebrated over Easter when sin and death were conquered forever. We have a God who is not only sovereign, but understands and uses suffering. And the Holy Spirit within every believer not just understands pain, but is experiencing it with us. You just can't get closer than that.

And yet, I seldom feel comforted. *What*?? Don't stop reading! Let me explain. My definition of comfort would be the lessening or removal of my pain and sadness. That's *not* how God chooses to comfort me. However, he does not leave me with nothing. I am finding the promises in his Word to be so much more precious during this difficult journey. They reveal to me God's character and give me that sought-after "peace that passes all understanding." Just a few of my favorites:

- "... it is the LORD your God who goes with you. He will not leave you or forsake you" (Deuteronomy 31:6).
- "Blessed are those who mourn for they shall be comforted" (Matthew 5:4).
- "The Lord is near to the brokenhearted and saves the crushed in spirit" (Psalm 34:18).
- "... and, lo, I am with you always, even unto the end of the world. Amen" (Matthew 28:20).
- "You have kept count of my tossings; put my tears in your bottle" (Psalm 56:8).
- "Come to me, all who are weary and heavy laden, and I will give you rest" (Matthew 11:28).

- "In this world you will have tribulation, but take heart, I have overcome the world" (John 16:33).

The other way I see and feel God's comfort is from the blessings he drops into my life, sometimes completely unexpectedly. I'm so grateful for the friends and family who have walked through this difficult journey with me. I promised in an earlier blog that I would share some of the ways I have been blessed thus far, so here you go:

- Two friends who text me hugs *Every. Single. Day.*
- The neighbor up the street who, upon just learning of Dale's death, showed up on my doorstep Valentine's Day morning with a bouquet of flowers and said, "I thought Dale would want you to have these."
- The friend who regularly sends me a text with the simple words, "How R U doing?"
- The friends who have stayed on the phone with me for hours as I've shared whatever pain I was going through that day. Or who were willing to listen as I talked about my life with Dale.
- The friends who have blessed me with vacation getaways to lift my spirits. (That's right – I have those kinds of friends, too!)
- Friends who have called me when they felt the Holy Spirit nudging them, just to check in.
- Those who took the initiative to set up coffee, lunch, or dinner dates.
- Friends who didn't give up the first time I turned them down because I just didn't have the strength that day.
- The nurse who prayed for me just this week in the doctor's office. And she wasn't praying for my cholesterol levels!
- Those who sent me words of encouragement or understanding through the mail, email, text, or Facebook. They truly brightened my day and reminded me of all those who care about me.

There are many more examples of what I call "nuggets from heaven" that God drops in my every day. I'm learning to recognize them for the blessings they are and to be thankful that God loves me enough to comfort me in such a personal way.

This really just scratches the surface of all I've taken in over the past six months since Dale's death. But I trust that it hits the big issues and gives you a glimpse into this world and takes away a little bit of the mystique of widowhood!

While on the surface the hard lessons and the encouraging lessons may seem to be opposite ends of the spectrum, I believe they really are all tied together. God uses the depth and the length of my pain to refine me, through this fire, into the person he wants me to become - a woman who can have a greater impact on those around her and ultimately on God's kingdom. How could I possibly want anything less than that?

"The Last of the Firsts"

Day 365

That's right. It has now been one full year since Dale died last October 16. And that means I've also gone through his first birthday, the first Thanksgiving, the first Christmas, the first New Year's, the first Easter, my first birthday, the first Father's Day, and our first wedding anniversary without him. And now, the first anniversary of his death.

How does one even begin to capture all that entails, all that I've grieved through, all that I've learned, all the blessings God continues to bestow on me? I know I can only do it with God giving me the words to say and the messages he wants me to share. Grab a tissue, here we go ...

I learned a management technique many years ago called The Oreo Principle. It stated that, if you had to share a criticism with someone, you should sandwich it between two layers of praise. It is still very wise counsel, and I thought it would be an appropriate framework for this anniversary post.

So, I promise to start and end with good things. But reality isn't all happiness and puppy dog tails, so the middle "layer" will be the gut-wrenching stuff that continues to be true for me. And I would do a disservice if I didn't honestly represent that middle layer along with the outer ones. Part of helping a grieving friend is acknowledging the depth of the hurt. So I'm not mincing words there.

But, let me be clear, the good stuff is also true for me. I have found that the times of joy and blessing (yes, I do have them) are unaffected by times of deep grieving. Just as those times of grieving are not lessened by my times of happiness.

If this were a Venn diagram, the circles wouldn't even touch! Both are entirely true in my daily life and seem to coexist as completely separate entities, unaffected by the other. Or I might say, completely separate layers of the cookie!

Layer One – Blessings

- I have learned to rely on God's strength and promises during these difficult days.
- My faith has grown in leaps and bounds as God opens my eyes to new truths about his character.
- God has dropped countless "nuggets from heaven" into my days to remind me that he loves me.
- Scripture has come alive as it goes from head knowledge to heart knowledge.
- I have gained new friendships – in some cases with others who are grieving their own losses.
- Some existing friendships have deepened significantly as they stepped into this grief with me.
- I have made my bed *Every. Single. Day*!
- I have been blessed by the friends who continue to be there for me, reaching out daily in some cases, hurting with me, praying for me, and loving me.
- Family relationships have been healed.
- I'm living a "fairly normal life"...
- I've read some incredible books and devotionals highlighting all the ways that God works *through* our pain and suffering, giving me invaluable insights.
- I've been on several trips that have brightened my days, a couple compliments of some awesome friends.
- The household has a new four-legged blessing named Winnie!
- I am wiser, and deeper.
- I have never been angry with God, and I still trust him completely.
- My longing for heaven has increased exponentially!
- I have *amazing* memories from the past 35 years that warm my heart and remind me how very blessed I am to have had a relationship like I had with Dale. Faithful and loving till the end.
- I *will* see him again.

Layer Two – Grief

- This is unquestionably the most difficult year I have ever experienced in my life.
- I have cried for 365 consecutive days ... and counting.
- The days are actually getting harder, not easier.
- I'm beginning to understand why so many widows say that the second year of widowhood is so much harder than the first.
- I miss Dale more now than six months ago.
- I have lost friends.
- I now know what it means to experience waves of sadness.
- There is an element of sadness in every day.
- I have never been so lonely.
- Even though the memories are precious, I am often inundated with them when I least expect it and they almost always lead to tears.
- There are no shortcuts to healing. And it's out of my control.
- Despite the "fairly normal life" mentioned in Layer One, there is very little about my life that feels normal.
- I think a broken heart is a physical reality. Mine feels broken.
- I believe there are parts of me that will never heal. I will always have a hole in my soul.
- Heaven seems so far off.

Layer Three – Hope and Purpose

Lately I've begun telling people that I'm living a double life. One is exemplified by Layer Two. And the other is where I clearly hear God's call.

Over the past several decades, I often wondered if God might have a ministry for me one day when I was alone. Little did I know it would be the direct result of my husband's death.

And yet, I think it would be fair to say that I am *excited* about this ministry calling. And the heart of it? To teach others how to be a blessing to their grieving friend.

I know that nearly everyone struggles with what to say, what to do, what *not* to say or do when a friend suffers a deep loss. I've been there. And now I'm on the other side. God is calling me to use this new-found knowledge to help others be that blessing.

At the risk of sounding cheesy, I feel that all my career and life experiences have prepared me for this new chapter in my life. I just didn't know it until now.

God has essentially "cleared my plate" so that my life focus can now be on this ministry. I'm energized by it, but also overwhelmed by it! I'm not used to a world that includes SEO, headshots, metadata, and branding. But God is bringing the right people into my life to help me navigate this new world. I even have a board of directors! (Sorry, sometimes you just can't take the "corporate" out of the career woman.)

There's so much more I could tell you, but suffice it to say, stay tuned for an official ministry launch, including a new website/blog, soon. I genuinely believe God has big things planned and I am honored and humbled to be used by him.

So, that's the whole cookie! Thank you for traveling this journey with me thus far. Honestly, I think it's just begun, and I can't wait to see what's ahead. Somehow, I believe Dale also has a sense of what's happening and is my biggest cheerleader from above.

"For I know the plans I have for you," declares the Lord,
"plans to prosper you and not to harm you, plans to
give you hope and a future."
Jeremiah 29:11

"Widowhood 2.0"

Day 394

I have now entered the infamous and much-dreaded second year of widowhood. Are you surprised by that? Being curious about the subject, I Googled "second year of widowhood" a few months ago.

Oh my, there is *much* written on this subject, and everything I read was written by someone who was walking right in the middle of it. Unfortunately, it's a pretty well-kept secret.

But I can't say I was completely surprised by this. I do think I entered this stage earlier than some, not because I'm trying to be an over-achiever, but because I was already living alone and had been taking care of all the household responsibilities for about four years prior to Dale's death. I'd already experienced some "widow-like" circumstances.

I decided to Google this topic once more before starting this blog post, to be more intentional about what was being shared. (I also found that many of the women commenting on these blogs had *also* Googled this topic!)

Here are some of the most prevalent emotions and experiences expressed by the many women whose words I read:

Year One

- Loneliness sets in
- Numb
- Shock
- Survival
- Acute pain
- Going through the motions
- Handling the necessary details of death
- Taking on new roles
- Strong support system

Year Two

- LONELIER!
- Harder than Year One (everyone said this)
- Chronic
- Visceral
- Permanent
- Weaker support system
- Disappointed reality – he's not coming back
- It's not getting better
- This is my life now
- Begin living without him

If years one and two were doors in a gameshow, would you really want to choose either one of them? Definitely not!

Do I relate to these Year Two emotions? To a very great extent, yes, I do. And have since about the eight-month mark when I felt bombarded by so many memories that brought me to tears. Much more than in the first six months.

Here are some additional heartaches I struggle with:

- I'm conflicted between wanting people to still check in on me – and yet not wanting to still need it.
- I'm tired of daily crying, but part of me doesn't want to lose that emotional connection to Dale.
- My go-to person for all the joys and sorrows in my life isn't here anymore. I can't take this deep sorrow and increasing loneliness to him. And that is an ache that continues to grow the longer I'm without him.

But, if you've been following any of this blog over the past months, you know that I am not without hope, and I am not unaware of the blessings in my life.

It bears repeating – God is my all-sufficiency in this trial. And not just for the gut-wrenching first few weeks. He's here for the long haul. And honestly, the long haul is essentially until I leave this earth.

Widowhood isn't a condition you eventually get over. It is something you learn how to live with for the rest of your life. You are forever changed by it. Kind of like having a limb amputated. You *always* know it's not there anymore, but you figure out how to do life without it.

So, I guess the goal of this post is really two-fold. First, I wanted to shed some light on what this journey is like, even past that "magical" (not …) first year mark.

Secondly, I wanted you to know that my strength and my hope is still rooted in my heavenly Father and his Son, Jesus.

- He is the same today, yesterday and forever (Hebrews 13:8).
- He will never leave me or forsake me (Deuteronomy 31:6). He collects my tears in His bottle (Psalm 56:8).
- And because of these promises, I can count it all joy (James 1:2).

Here's to a year of learning deeper truths from God, no matter how my heart is doing.

"Yet this I call to mind and therefore I have hope:
Because of the Lord's great love we are not consumed,
for his compassions never fail.
They are new every morning; great is your faithfulness."
Lamentations 3:21-23

"Scars vs. Scabs"

Day 729

Tomorrow marks two years since I lost Dale. Ironically, he isn't actually lost. I know he's enjoying perfection in heaven and for that I'm enormously grateful.

There are so many directions I could take with this post. So much to share in the two years since my world changed. I want to be true to the purpose of this ministry - which is in great part to enlighten, educate, and encourage people as they strive to help their hurting friend.

But part of that process is to also understand more fully what someone is experiencing in their grief or pain. So I will attempt to address both goals.

First, the personal side of things. It absolutely blows my mind that Dale has been gone for two years. So often, it seems like yesterday. And, honestly? Sometimes it feels like I haven't really healed much at all.

Oh sure, I might look pretty normal if you see me on the street, but I'm still raw on the inside. Every day still includes sadness and loneliness, and tears still come almost daily.

And yet, I am functioning most of the time. You know the usual – eating, sleeping, exercising, socializing, praying. I'm grateful for all that I've learned through this trial, and for how I've seen God so clearly move. This ministry gives me a purpose that I wouldn't have if Dale were still alive. Interesting trade-off, isn't it?

That's really all the space I want to devote to my personal journey over the past two years.

What I'd rather do, is give my readers a visual that helps illustrate the unique nature of widowhood, in my case, or any long-term tragic loss someone may be suffering.

Hence, the title – Scars vs. Scabs. Sounds like a medical flag football game, doesn't it? Yuck!

We often hear about the scars someone bears from emotional traumas. And we also talk about broken hearts healing over time. Even with complete healing, a scar remains. Any trial or loss we suffer through almost always results in a scar. We are changed, for better or worse, by the trials we experience in this life.

I feel scars from the deaths of both of my parents, of good friends I've lost through the years, and of all the relatives in my parents' generation. Every one of you bears scars from *something* in your past. Maybe it was abuse, maybe losses like mine, maybe personal tragedies that you've mostly moved past.

The scar is a reminder that you've been hurt, but you are now essentially healed. Certainly not back to perfection. No, you are forever changed by the trauma, but it doesn't devastate your life anymore. When you look at your scar, it reminds you of what you've experienced and how far you've come.

A scab, however, is quite a different "condition." It's headed toward healing, but any little bump or scrape will cause it to bleed again and the healing process starts over a couple of steps back.

My healing stage is a scab. Maybe it will be a scar someday. Maybe not. What bumps into my scab that makes it start bleeding again?

- A song on the radio
- A date on the calendar that's gone from joyous to heartbreaking
- A memory that hits when I least expect it
- A plumbing problem that now needs a professional to fix
- A picture that takes me back to our better days
- The empty side of the bed
- Weddings
- Funerals
- Activities that fit couples best
- Lonely days and night
- Putting up Christmas lights

The list isn't all-inclusive. There are reminders and "bumps" in most days and that list would be much too long to include here. That's not the important part of this message.

It's to understand the differences between scars and scabs – and more accurately, where someone's healing might be along that spectrum. Or at a minimum, just recognizing that there *is* a spectrum!

My guess is that, upon deeper reflection, you too can likely identify scars and scabs in your own lives. Or in the lives of your family and friends.

So, just what are the take-aways from this post? Perhaps a greater awareness of the people in your life who are struggling to move their wounds from scabs to scars. Maybe the acknowledgment that some scabs never heal. Possibly even a greater understanding of your own wound status.

Action plan? Be kind. Almost everyone has a hidden wound. But mine's not hidden – I'm fortunate to analyze (and often treat) my wounds right here on this weekly post. Thanks for being part of my medical team!

"Put on then, as God's chosen ones, holy and beloved,
compassionate hearts, kindness, humility,
meekness, and patience."
Colossians 3:12

Wow! That was some journey, wasn't it? Admittedly, it was hard for me to read through them again and relive so much of what I was experiencing. But there are some basic themes that came through loudly and clearly.

- The pain of widowhood is relentless.
- God is sufficient.
- I'm becoming a different person through this season.
- My faith is deeper and more secure.
- There are blessings in every day.

It's not a bad list, overall! My prayer is that you can claim your own set of blessings from whatever trial you're experiencing. Ultimately, may your blessings outweigh your pain.

Matchless Nature of Wedding Day Memories

The fact that I've written three posts within two years related to the romance of marriage, points to the unique pain associated with that emotion. They are always some of the hardest days of the year for me.

"Wedding Day Memories and Lessons"

Day 346

Eleven months and 11 days ago, I was oddly grateful that it would be a long time before I had to "celebrate" our first wedding anniversary alone. Now, as I write this, it is a mere two days away and I've been in tears for the past few weeks, dreading the emotions of this day. Yes, September 27, 1986, was one of the very best days of my life. What day better represents your hopes and dreams as a married couple more than your wedding day?

We lived in the Twin Cities area at the time; me on the St. Paul side and Dale on the Minneapolis side. We were in the process of building a home on an acreage north of Stillwater, MN, where we would live for the next five and a half years.

My across-the-alley neighbor at the time had told me about the venue his daughter had gotten married on and I immediately thought it would be such a cool idea! So, we celebrated our wedding with a four-hour cruise on the Jonathan Padelford Riverboat on the Mississippi River, out of The Port of St. Paul, with about 90 of our friends and family members. God bless our pastor for signing on for that kind of commitment!

It was a beautiful, sunny September day and it was all that a bride could dream of and more. After the ceremony, we had a live band to dance the evening away to and everyone had a grand old time! A white limousine picked us up when we returned to port and we enjoyed a fun tour around the lakes in Minneapolis. Truly a dream-come-true kind of day and I'm so grateful for all those memories that make me smile 32 years later.

As I thought through the memories of that day and all the joy that it held, I didn't want this post to *just* be about those memories. I wanted to share another truth and an inside look, if you will, about this grieving process. Sorry to be a Debbie Downer, but let's face it, days like this are bittersweet.

Think with me, for a moment, of the greatest love of your life. It could be your spouse – especially back on your wedding day. It might be the love you felt when your children were born. Maybe it's the love you had for a parent or a grandparent or a sibling or a best friend. Maybe even a beloved pet.

For me, there's no question that the greatest, deepest love of my life was, and still is, Dale. Have you decided who *your* greatest love is? Don't read on until you have!

Now, let me ask you this, "Was there *anything* you could have done to change the way you felt about that person at that point in your life?" I'm quite certain your answer would be a resounding NO! That kind of love is so powerful that no amount of sheer will could have dimmed its radiance in your life.

The parallel I want to draw for you now is this: Just like there was *nothing* I could do to change how deep my love was for Dale on that special day 32 years ago, there is now *nothing* I can do to change the depth of my grief for him now that he is gone. They are directly linked.

Let that sink in for a moment. I'm sure the first reaction for some of you might be to dispute that or talk me out of feeling that way. Surely, I must be able to do *something* to move past all this pain. Well, I'm doing all the things I "should" during this grieving period. I'm eating healthy (mostly), I'm sleeping well, I'm exercising daily, I'm engaged in normal life activities, I'm praying to God.

And yet, the pain and sorrow and grieving remain. Healing will never come from my own hand or will. It will be a function of time, to a certain degree. And ultimately, it will come as I continue to rely on God's hand leading me through this dark time.

So, my message to you, dear readers, is this: Whether you understand it or agree with it or not, just trust me when I tell you that lessening or eliminating this heartache is as out of my control today as changing my love for Dale would have been 32 years ago.

If you doubt that, go back to that love you were remembering just a few minutes ago. Can't change it, can you? That's the message. That's the lesson.

So, what's your takeaway? Don't rush someone through their grieving process. Don't tell them to move on. Don't expect normalcy – and don't let it fool you if you see it.

Cry with them. Grieve with them. Extend kindness and grace and understanding. Be a blessing to your grieving friend.

"My flesh and my heart may fail, but God is the strength of my heart and my portion forever."
Psalm 73:26

"You're Still the One"

Day 486

Every now and then, my country music roots show up in a blog post. Usually accompanied by an apology to those of you who aren't fans! So, I'm sorry ... again.

Now many of you would probably place Shania Twain in some sort of cross-over category and that's fine. Back in 1997 I purchased her newly released album entitled, *Come On Over*, and proceeded to listen to all the cuts on the album.

When I got to the song, "You're Still the One," I immediately thought, "*This* is *our* song!" So, I excitedly called Dale into the kitchen and told him to listen to this because it was *our* song! Yes, I did feel strongly about that. Dale wasn't quite as "over the moon" as I was, but did agree that it represented our relationship well.

One section of the song talks about how the featured couple was told that they weren't likely to

"make it" for the long haul. Their response is that they're glad they didn't listen to these nay-sayers, are grateful they beat the odds, and are still going strong. That was us!

As you can imagine, our 20-year age difference caused many to question just how long this relationship would last. I found out years after our wedding that one of my aunts said this to another relative *on our wedding day*, "I'll give it a year."

Honestly, it just makes me chuckle now after our 31-year marriage. A few years into that marriage, this same aunt, who has since passed away, would often write to me and include this in her letters, "Say hi to the noble Dale." So, whenever I passed the greeting along, he'd say, "That's a good thing, right?" Yes, honey, that's a very good thing – especially coming from my very happily single Aunt Margaret.

So, why write about this now? Well, for some reason this song from 20-some years ago has been getting some play time on my country radio station over the past couple of weeks. And it's made its way back into my psyche a bit – with a mixture of warm fuzzies for the joy of experiencing that together, and heartache over the loss of that kind of love.

So on this Valentine's Day, celebrating all things "love," I'd like to once again claim this as *our* song. Despite all that we've gone through, and all the emptiness from these past 16 months, I can still, without hesitation say to Dale, "You're still the one." Thank you, God, for blessing me with a love like that.

I pray that somewhere in your life, you, too, have experienced that kind of love. If not with a spouse, then through the love of Jesus, which is greater than anything we humans can muster up in our own strength. Ultimately, *he*, Jesus, is the one.

"So now faith, hope, and love abide, these three;
but the greatest of these is love."
1 Corinthians 13:13

"It Was the Best of Times; It Was the Worst of Times"

Day 607

For those of you who are "literature literate," you will recognize these words as the beginning of Charles Dickens' famous *Tale of Two Cities."* I read it way back in sophomore year English class in high school.

While these words are renowned, I applied them very appropriately to my college years. No question, at the time, that's exactly how I described my college experience to everyone! For me, it absolutely was the best of times and the worst of times. But that was [cough, cough] years ago.

I was honored to play the piano for a wedding today. It was a beautiful event - full of hope, full of love, full of gospel teaching, full of joy, and full of possibilities.

It's the first wedding I've attended since Dale's death 20 months ago (tomorrow). But it wasn't my first invitation. I haven't been able to attend alone yet. This was easier because I camped out at the keyboard throughout the ceremony. I had other things to keep my mind occupied. And I made it through without losing it. Yea me!

Afterwards, I was chatting with a friend and mentioned that this was my first wedding outing post-Dale. I commented that weddings were harder for me than funerals. I've attended several funerals in those 20 months and, while they're never a joyous event, for some reason, they didn't elicit any additional sadness as a widow.

I continued to explain to this friend that weddings were hard because our wedding day was the very best day of my marriage. My wedding was also a beautiful event – full of hope, full of love, not-quite-as-full of gospel teaching, full of joy, and full of possibilities.

That is what makes attendance at a wedding so hard for me as a widow now. I can't help but be transported back to that amazing day in September 1986. What a blessing that my memory of that day is still so crystal clear. And not just the memory of the activities of the day, but the memory of all the emotions I felt so many years ago.

With 32 years in the rear-view mirror, I can see the mixture of what our marriage was. Certainly, it was times of hope, love, joy, and possibilities. But it was also times of trials, challenges, selfishness, and heartache. That's exactly what marriage is – and that's what this beautiful young couple will grow to understand over time. Marriage – and life – are a mixture of joy and sorrow.

So, back to my conversation with my friend. As we wrapped it up, I said, "Weddings are hard because mine was the best day of my life. And Dale's funeral was the worst day of my life."

Ta-da – *Tale of Two Cities*! Tale of life in this world. But that's okay because what's ahead for us as believers is an *incredibly* beautiful event – *full* of love, *full* of the Gospel (because Jesus will be there), *full* of joy, and *full* of eternal joy. Hope will be fulfilled.

So for those of you who are married, whether it's three hours as this young couple – or 50 years, hug your spouse, tell them you love them and thank God for the work he does through your marriage.

I miss Dale every day, but I'm so grateful not only for that special day 32 years ago, but for the journey that brought me from wedding day to funeral day and beyond. This is life. Embrace it all. The best of times and the worst of times.

"So also you have sorrow now, but I will see you again, and your hearts will rejoice, and no one will take your joy from you."
John 16:22

Thank you for walking through these milestone blog posts with me. If you are grieving a loss right now, I hope they encouraged you to keep fighting the good fight, and looking for the blessings in your days. If you're just looking for a deeper understanding of this process, then I hope you came away wiser!

And so "the honest griever" begins marking those bittersweet milestones.

8

Helpful Resources

As I wrap up this Daily Grind section, I want to encourage you by providing some resources I have found helpful as I've walked this difficult road. Some of the books and devotionals were recommended or given to me; others just "happened" to show up in my reading suggestions for the day.

Written Words and the Written "Word"

This isn't merely a chapter about book titles. I want to look at a variety of resources that may be helpful to you. So, let me start with the best resource ever written – the Bible, God's Word to us here on earth. You don't have to question if the author's theology is correct or not – the words are divinely inspired by God himself. And if you are a believer, the Holy Spirit within you can lead you to the scriptures you need that day *and* help enlighten you as you read through them. That is the same Spirit that is walking with you on this journey. He knows better than anyone *exactly* what you're going through, unlike people who might suggest they do!

There is no greater resource to fill you with hope, or encourage you about the future, or give you examples of people who have overcome great tragedies, or even give you permission to cry and to grieve. *Everything* you need is in God's Word. Hands down, it's the first and best resource.

If you're like me, you know a lot of scripture texts, but maybe can't remember just where to find them! I hate to admit this, but Google has been a great help as I've searched for specific scripture verses. It can be as simple as searching for "scripture verses about comfort." Or fill in the blank!

Over the past few years, and especially when I'm walking Daisy, my Frenchie/Boston mix, God often gives me insights into what my walk with *him* should look like. So, in an effort to capture just a bit of his imparted wisdom, I've written a 14-day devotional which you can download for free with the link at the end of the book. I hope and pray that some of these insights will be helpful to you, regardless of where you are on your journey.

I've alluded to a few of the written resources in some of the posts, but I'd like to expound on them a bit and tell you what they've meant to me.

- ***Heaven*** by Randy Alcorn (Tyndale Momentum, 2011) – It ranks at or near the top of my favorite books ever! This is the best resource I've read about the nitty-gritty details of what heaven will be like – and more specifically, what the new earth will be like once Jesus returns. He answers tons of questions you may have about heaven with a straight-forward, biblically-based approach. And most importantly, it offers such wonderful hope of eternity with Jesus.
- ***If God is Good – Faith in the Midst of Suffering and Evil*** by Randy Alcorn (Multnomah, 2014) – Same author, *very* different subject matter. This is *not* an easy read. I've read it twice and I still need to reread certain sections. But, in typical Alcorn style, he digs deep into the subject matter and helps us understand a biblical perspective of why this world has so much suffering in it. And then shows us example after example of how God worked incredible *good* from those devastating losses.
- ***Walking with God through Pain and Suffering*** by Timothy Keller (Penguin Books, 2015) – Similar subject as the previous book and includes a look at how Christianity compares with all the other world religions, and how it is the *only* faith that truly has an answer for suffering. Fun fact – this book showed up in the daily email I get from BookBubs at the perfect time when I needed this reminder. Thank you, God!
- ***Streams in the Desert*** with numerous contributors (Zondervan, rev. 1999) – This was a gift from a dear friend in the first few weeks after Dale's death. I am now on my *third* time through it! Every single day of this year-long devotional is filled with new ways to look at how God is our strength in whatever desert we find ourselves. Deep and creative insights that have sustained me time and time again.
- ***The Undistracted Widow – Living for God after Losing Your Husband*** by Carol W. Cornish (Crossway, 2010) – I *love* this book! Carol is a solid biblical teacher who lost her husband of 38 years. She delves into how to look at this new role we can play as widows in God's army. I found it extremely practical – and even felt that she spoke my heart

many times on difficult positions I've taken in my widowhood. (Look for more on this in the "To Marry or Not to Marry" chapter.)

- ***The Hurt and the Healer*** by Andrew Farley and Bart Millard (Baker Books, 2013) – If you're a fan of the Christian singing group, MercyMe, you'll probably recognize that this title is also the title of one of their hit songs. I found some unique suggestions for looking at how we can heal from hurts.

Music and Emotional Healing

And speaking of songs, I found so many that I would sing and cry along with. There are artists out there who have also suffered losses, who long for heaven, who cry out to God with their questions. Putting those emotions to music for all of us to experience is a powerful way to grieve and process through these challenging times. I'm grateful for the role they played, and continue to play in my healing.

True confessions – I'm a *huge* MercyMe fan and was blessed to go to one of their concerts about six months after Dale's death. I had purchased their most recent album, *Lifer*, along with their greatest hits album. So many of their songs sustained me during those days. Here are my favorites from MercyMe.

- "I Can Only Imagine" (*I Can Only Imagine,* Ino/Epic, 2001)
- "Even If" (*Lifer,* Fair Trade/Columbia, 2017)
- "Hurt and the Healer" (*Hurt and the Healer,* Fair Trade/Columbia, 2012)
- "Bring the Rain" (*I Can Only Imagine – Best of MercyMe,* Fair Trade/Columbia, 2018)
- "Homesick" (*I Can Only Imagine – Best of MercyMe,* Fair Trade/Columbia, 2018)
- "Almost Home" (Fair Trade/Columbia, 2019)

I do enjoy a few other artists as well. Here are some I highly recommend crying along with!

- "Praise You in This Storm" by Casting Crowns (*Lifesong,* Reunion Records, 2005)
- "Well Done" by The Afters (*The Afters,* Fair Trade/Columbia, 2019)
- "Yes, I Will" by Vertical Worship (*Bright Faith Bold Future,* Essential Worship, 2018)
- "The Other Side" by Colton Dixon (*Identity,* Sparrow, 2017)

Filling my quiet moments with music and solid literature was one of the most important parts of my healing. And each format brought its own benefits. The music helped bring the pain to the surface where God could do his cleansing work. *So* much better than keeping it buried and ignored.

The books gave me new insights into the promises of God and the way he continues to work in my life for my good. I can't overstate how important it is to have a solid understanding of who God is when the storms hit. We need more than our fickle feelings to get us through. We need solid food from God's Word and from biblical scholars who can provide additional insights.

Regardless of the avenue or genre you choose, finding an outlet that helps you heal either through emotions or intellect, or both, is vital to your healing process.

Let's Talk

Another resource that I personally did not use, but which can be extremely effective is grief support groups. I often felt that sharing my heart and my heartache through my blog was my alternative to counseling! I also had new widow friends who helped me process the deep emotions I was experiencing.

Even though I was grateful for friends who had walked this "widow road," I found that non-widow friends could be just as comforting. I wasn't looking for someone to fix my pain. I just needed friends who would listen to me, without judgment, as I processed through it.

So, I can't speak from personal experience as to the benefits of working through grief in a support group. But I have friends who have found great healing within their group. Feeling free to express whatever heartache you're experiencing, especially with people who are grieving with you, is a wonderful gift. Knowing you're not alone in the crazy thoughts and emotions you're experiencing is invaluable.

What resource you find most helpful isn't as important as making sure that you have *something*. God has not created us to thrive outside of community, so going it alone during one of the most difficult seasons of your life is a recipe for deeper heartache. So please find an outlet for your pain. Talk to a counselor, a pastor, a friend, your dog. Write through your heartache. Read about biblical examples of those who emerged victorious on the other side of their struggles. Find good books and/or good music to express the emotions that only your heart knows. You are not alone.

And so "the honest griever" finds solace and healing through God-designed resources.

SECTION III

The Nature of Grief

The dictionary defines grief as "deep sorrow, especially that caused by someone's death." Eight little words to describe a phenomenon unlike anything most people will experience in their lifetimes. Hardly seems adequate, does it? So, as "the honest griever," I feel a responsibility to fill in those gaping holes a bit.

This section will delve deeply into many facets of grief; why we have it, how we can describe it (in more than eight words), what are its characteristics, and why it's so important that we don't ignore it. The view begins broadly and then the focus becomes narrower as we zero in on the unique nature of grief in an individual's life.

9

Why Grief?

An excellent question! Wouldn't this be a much better world if we didn't have to deal with grief on any level or in any form? Silly question. Of course, a life without pain would be better than one with it. Duh! So the answer to the "why grief" question demands that we look past the grief itself, and focus on what happened to bring grief into this world.

When Grief Entered Our World

Let's go *way* back to the creation story in Genesis. I'll just hit the highlights for you in the interest of space. And the fact that it's all perfectly recorded already. When God created the universe and all that's in it, after seven days, he rested and called all his creation "good," except for one piece. After "God created man in his own image, in the image of God he created him; male and female he created them," he called that portion of his work, "very good." We humans are the crowning jewel in God's creation.

After God created Adam, and then Eve from Adam's rib, they lived in perfect harmony with God and the rest of creation in the Garden of Eden. It was paradise in every sense of the word. It's what we just wished for in that first paragraph. But that's not nearly the end of the story, even though the *real* end of the story will look very much like that. You'll have to wait for a later chapter for that Good News.

Back to the Garden of Eden. This perfect existence was disrupted when Satan, in the form of a serpent, led Adam and Eve down a dangerous path. He convinced them that God was keeping things from them, and of course they could eat of the God-forbidden Tree of the Knowledge of Good and Evil. Satan said God just wanted to keep that all for himself.

Satan convinced them that they could be like God if they ate the forbidden fruit. So Eve took a bite from that infamous fruit and offered one to Adam.

Enter disobedience. Enter sin. Enter separation from God. Enter the fact that God's perfect creation became tainted by this first act of defiance against a holy God. So, from this point on, sin would taint *everything* including the world into which every human being was born, and every human being.

As if separation from God wasn't enough, guess what else entered the world. Suffering, loss, trials, heartache, death, and ... *grief. This* answers the question, "Why grief?" It wasn't part of God's original perfect plan. But he does have the perfect solution to set everything right again. It's in the person of his only Son, Jesus. As promised, I'll share more about the Good News in the last section.

Meanwhile, all of mankind will suffer through the consequences God imposed back in that garden. But he doesn't let it consume us. He also fills our earthly lives with blessings galore and hope for our future.

Joy and Sorrow Co-Existing

Before I share a blog post I wrote on this whole "sin-tainting" concept, I want to share an important lesson I learned in those first months after Dale died. Joy and sorrow can absolutely co-exist. I've been living that life for years now.

I have moments where I feel incredibly blessed by God, moments when I enjoy deep fellowship and laughter with friends, moments where God feels so close to me. And yet, I can turn right around and have a major meltdown because *something* triggered it when I least expected it. I'm overwhelmed once again with tears and sorrow and heartache.

My good times don't diminish my pain, but neither does the sorrow steal my joy. We can have both. And while the joy doesn't eliminate that pain, I've found that it provides a healthy balance in my daily life.

So, until God sets this aright, we will live in this world that, sadly, includes a healthy dose of grief.

And so "the honest griever" experiences the ramifications of The Fall in deeper ways than ever before.

"Sin Taints ... Everything"

Day 450

During this past year, I've come across so many pictures from my life with Dale. Some came in sympathy cards, some came from family, many were here in the house and just rediscovered as I go through Dale's "space." Some are just of him, but so many are of the two of us as early as our dating years.

I can't help but notice how very young and "in our prime" we look! In many cases they are a stark contrast to the reality of those last few years together as he failed physically and mentally. And honestly, I'm no spring chicken either!

I often joke with friends that when I see Dale in heaven one day, I want him to look like he did on our wedding day, not on the day he died. And I want to look like I did in those early days, too.

All of this reminded me of a very real, but sorrowful truth. From the day we are born, we are dying. Aren't I just a ray of sunshine? But all we need to do is look around us to acknowledge this reality. Of course, our bodies are falling apart to one degree or another. The seasons remind us that much of nature goes through this death cycle. The Second Law of Thermodynamics states that the universe tends toward disorder.

And most powerfully, the death of loved ones reminds us of the mortal nature of this world.

Sometimes I think we take this inevitability so for granted that we forget its source. It happened back in the Garden of Eden when Adam and Eve sinned, and the course of mankind was set forever – until we die, or Jesus comes back.

Trust me, this will not be a dissertation on sin and its effects, but suffice it to say that everything in the heavens and earth was tainted and headed for decay and death from that point on. We often spend much of our later lives fighting this reality and the cosmetic and Botox industries thank us very much!

But don't we all long for the days of our prime? Doesn't it seem to be an innate desire in our souls? Ecclesiastes tells us that God has placed eternity in our hearts, and I believe it only makes sense that we want to be young and vibrant in eternity!

That is speculation on my part, so don't go looking for scripture to support that word for word. But we do know that God will make all things new one day. We just can't know exactly what that looks like in this life.

Not only do I look forward to the day when we can be rid of these deteriorating physical bodies, but I also long to be rid of the sin that lurks around all my thoughts, desires, words, and actions. Talk about breaking free from our bonds! What a glorious day for us to anticipate if we are believers.

I think that may be one of the reasons why I don't spend much energy on memories from my life with Dale that showcase those sins. I don't want to dwell on the times our pride or stubbornness or insecurities or frailties created difficult memories.

I want to camp out on the very best moments of our very best days. In short, I want to remember those times that, in retrospect, seem near perfect to me. Naïve? Perhaps.

As I worked through this thought process over the past few months, I concluded that what I'm longing for physically, emotionally, mentally, and spiritually is … *heaven*!

Full disclosure – I am studying Randy Alcorn's book, *Heaven*, (Tyndale Momentum, 2011) (for the third time) and that is definitely influencing my thought processes lately. But the promises in God's Word are true and, as believers, we *can* look forward to a future eternity that is free from physical decay, or any other encumbrance that sin has saddled us with in this life.

Restoration of everything that's tainted in our earthly lives is an incredible hope we can cling to. I honestly don't know if it's wrong to create these rose-colored memories of my time with Dale. But it feels like a comforting way to bridge that gap until I step into eternity.

"And he who was seated on the throne said,
'Behold, I am making all things new.'
Also he said, 'Write this down, for
these words are trustworthy and true.'"
Revelation 21:5

10

Grief Analogies

Grief is such an elusive topic that people through the ages have tried to describe and explain it in some highly creative ways. The myriad explanations out there speak to our desire to put grief in a well-defined box and wield some level of control over it. And yet, most of us realize that no amount of analogy-drawing will ease the pain. The best we can hope for is that it provides a new way of understanding this perplexing and complex emotion.

There is something in every one of these analogies that spoke into my own grief, helping me to understand it a little more clearly. I hope you find at least one that speaks to your heart, in whatever grief you're suffering through.

Sliding Scale of Grief

I alluded to this in an earlier blog post, but I'd like to camp out here a little longer and add some meat to the bones. Every day for the past two and a half years, I've had some level of grief in my life. Every. Single. Day. Let's say we have a scale that goes from zero to 100, with zero indicating not a shred of sadness in that day. The 100 on the other end of the scale suggests you're sobbing in bed for the entire day.

I, fortunately *and* unfortunately, never achieved either end of that spectrum! What I did experience, however, was a lot of sliding back and forth between both ends. Even in those early days, I was blessed with wonderful times that could even fill most of a day. Maybe I was spending it with a group of friends or having a heart-to-heart with just one good friend. Perhaps I was attending a concert or other "distracting" event that allowed me to forget the heartache for a few hours. That might help me hover for a while in the 10-20-point range, which was quite tolerable.

The next day might bring an onslaught of emotions because I was going through Dale's things or for no reason whatsoever. But the result was that I'd become overwhelmed with tears and heartache and find myself approaching 90 on the scale.

There was truly little rhyme or reason to it. And it wasn't a nice, neat straight line from 90 back down to 10. Picture a jagged mountain scene that a child might draw. That's what this would resemble. Very arbitrary and unpredictable, which added to the difficulty of the grief. I couldn't count on the days ahead to get progressively better. Maybe the two-year mark was better in some ways than day 30, but the road getting there was bumpy.

Waves of Grief

Nearly every grieving person I've talked with expresses their grief as coming in waves. When the loss first occurred, it was all I could do to keep my head above water. I was deep into the ocean amid lots of debris. Keeping afloat was the best I could hope for.

The waves were high and hit me at a dizzying pace. I'd have just barely grabbed a breath and the next waves would hit. What did I do when those waves hit me? Initially, curl up on the floor and sob, and wait for it to pass – usually when I was too exhausted to swim.

As time went by, admittedly most of the waves weren't quite as high and I had a little more time to catch my breath before the next one pounded into me. Yet, just as I thought I was figuring out the rhythm of the ocean, a tsunami wave would come crashing in and send me reeling.

At this stage, I don't have tsunami-size waves, or even large tidal waves hitting me regularly. Yes, they still can rise up when another storm roils the water – like writing this book! And, I'm never completely safe from the waves because, after all, my life is now spent in the ocean.

Amputated Limb

One of my favorite analogies, and I believe one of the clearest to comprehend, is to compare the loss of my spouse to the loss of a limb. I can just hear Dale saying to me, with a twinkle in his eye, "Is that really all I meant to you – an arm or a leg?"

In the early days after the amputation (read *death*), the pain is almost unbearable, and "pain meds" provide barely an ounce of relief. It's all-encompassing and consumes every waking moment. As some healing begins, there are moments when the pain becomes tolerable and you consider heading home from the hospital. But that infamous "phantom pain" that is so prevalent with amputations, also shows up in loss from death. It's not unusual to think you see your spouse as you go about your daily routine. Sadly, it's just someone who resembles him or her … again. Some widow(er)s tell me that they can even hear his or her voice occasionally.

As the "stump" heals, there is talk about adding a prosthetic arm or leg. Gee, not sure I'm quite ready for that today. It hurts to move on. Apparently, I haven't healed enough yet.

But eventually, enough healing does occur that we learn how to live without that essential limb. Maybe we've tried out the prosthetic. Or maybe we just hobble around and do the best we can. One thing is true – we are *always* aware that it's gone. We've just chosen to move forward without it because we must.

Fried Egg Model of Grief

I bet that heading piqued your curiosity a bit! When this concept was explained to me, I bought into the premise wholeheartedly, but until beginning this research, I had not heard that unique title. I like it!

Dr. Lois Tonkin is a lecturer, researcher, counsellor, and writer about loss and grief.[1] She is credited with coining this phrase and has been teaching this theory for over 20 years. The premise begins with how your life feels when grief initially overwhelms you. Draw a circle and shade it in completely. *This* is your life consumed with your pain.

As you begin the healing process and start venturing out into life again, the grief remains, but you now develop a life *around* that grief. So, continuing with the fried egg analogy, your grief is the yolk of the egg, and the life you attempt to live is the white of the egg growing around it.

It's really quite brilliant in its simplicity. And it hits on several relevant issues surrounding grief. First, the initial picture has only yolk. Grief permeates every aspect of your life at this stage. Secondly, this theory acknowledges that we never completely get over our grief. That yolk remains even as we step back into life. And lastly, it does allow for that re-entry back into the world. Growing a new life, so to speak, around the "grief yolk."

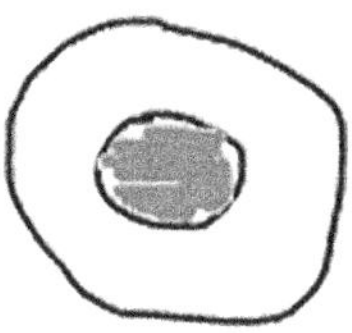

The Ball and the Box

A Canadian woman by the name of Lauren Herschel had a conversation with her doctor not long after losing her mother. She so appreciated how he explained grief to her that she sent a tweet out in December 2017 that has been retweeted almost 4,000 times! I had also heard this theory before knowing the history behind it and find it's another analogy that helps people understand the nature of grieving. I use it with her permission.

The pictures are the ones Lauren used in her tweet, with her apologies for not being an artist. I think she did great. Here's how Lauren explained it:

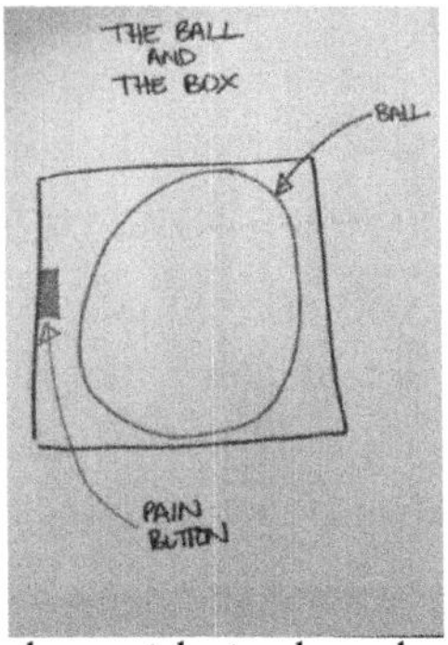

"There's a box with a ball in it. And a pain button. In the beginning, the ball is huge. You can't move the box without the ball hitting the pain button. It rattles around on its own in there and hits the button over and over. You can't control it - it just keeps hurting. Sometimes it seems unrelenting.

"Over time, the ball gets smaller. It hits the button less and less but when it does, it hurts just as much. It's better because you can function day to day more easily. But the downside is that the ball randomly hits that button when you least expect it."

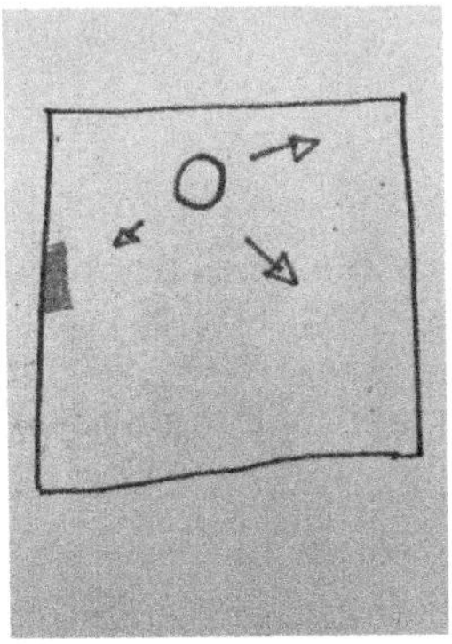

That's an interesting concept, isn't it? Again, hitting on some recurring themes we've shared in this chapter. The initially overwhelming nature of the grief, and then the eventual lessening of the pain. But it's always there and you never know what will hit the pain button, or when.

If you're currently grieving a deep loss, and maybe questioning why you can't seem to "get over this," or "move on," I hope these analogies will give you some comfort, knowing you aren't alone in your inability to get on with life. Because this grieving process is so complicated, it has resulted in people from across the globe searching for simple ways to illustrate its characteristics. I'm grateful for their insights.

If you haven't suffered a loss such as this, and are grappling with why a grieving friend in your life continues to struggle, I hope at least one of these examples will give you a glimpse into their world of hurt, and give you the compassion and empathy they need in their difficult days.

And so "the honest griever" looks for ways to understand the grieving process.

11

The Characteristics of Grief

As we move from the 30,000-foot view to a less lofty position, I'd like to share the characteristics of grief that I experienced personally, and often daily. One could fill up volumes with characteristics of grief, so I make no claims to be all-inclusive in this discussion. But the few I share here are the ones that rose to the top of the list as they infiltrated my days, and altered much of my life. Many of these experiences were chronicled by my personal blog posts, so I'll be sharing those "real-time" observations throughout this chapter.

While this is my list, I suspect that some or all of these characteristics would show up on the lists of many of you who are grieving your own loss.

Unique

Let's start by looking at the unique nature of grief. My own experience and the dozens of conversations I've had with other grievers make it clear that everyone has a unique journey. Grievers, this tells us we shouldn't be rattled by or stressed over the fact that Mrs. Smith and Mr. Jones had completely different experiences from ours.

Just like there are no identical snowflakes, there are no identical individuals (even identical twins have unique DNA), and hence *no* identical grief journeys. Yes, there may be similarities, and you can take some comfort in sharing those with other grieving people, but don't limit your grief by thinking it needs to fit a pre-conceived mold. I'll let this blog post from the ministry site speak in more detail about this important concept.

"Everyone's Journey is Unique"

Day 540

About a month ago, I posted a blog that talked about some specific things to say or avoid – and I promised a little more depth on some of those "statements to avoid." So, let's take a deeper look at this quite common statement: "I know [exactly] how you feel. I felt like that when …"

My noticeably short answer to that was, "No, you don't." Now I have the opportunity to explain why I believe this to be true. And just a reminder here – it's not necessary to know how the grieving person feels to be able to be a comfort to them. Listening and acknowledging their grief are two skills that can always serve you well.

So, just what is at the heart of this unique nature that I often allude to? I'd like to share what I experienced after the deaths of both of my parents to help illustrate my point.

I had wonderful parents. That's one of the blessings I'm most grateful for as I look back on my life. I loved them both and had a solid relationship with each of them – different, but very fulfilling.

My dad died very unexpectedly on January 1, 1992. He had a massive blood clot that covered all of one lung and half of the other. It had been forming for 12 weeks after minor prostate surgery. He was gone within 15 minutes of the onset with no warning whatsoever before that.

Dale and I lived in Stillwater, MN, at the time and I will never forget that phone call. His death absolutely rocked my world – and not in a good way. The Hoeksema side of the family usually lived well into their nineties so none of us was prepared for this.

Fast forward about 16 years. I had spent the past few years watching my sweet mom slowly disappear from the effects of dementia. When I walked into her nursing home room on December 23, 2007, I knew she wouldn't make it through the night. She died within a couple of hours of my arrival.

I grieved these two deaths very differently. But my *core* grief was the same. I was heartbroken to lose the parents that I dearly loved. That part of my grief looked very much the same.

With my dad's death, I struggled with the shock of losing him so unexpectedly. And everyone in the family and in the community was struggling with that as well.

There was no surprise with my mom's death, but what I *did* struggle with was the length of time I grieved her loss *before* her actual death.

My *core* grief was affected by the suddenness of my dad's death, and the long, lingering death of my mom.

That got me thinking about the myriad of circumstances affecting someone's grief – and how the totality of all those circumstances add up to make *everyone's journey unique.*

So, let's look at some of the ways our basic, core grieving can be altered by other factors. Here's a partial list, based on my experience personally, and from talking with many people about this subject. There's no doubt the list is much longer. Any one of you could add to it, based on what *you've* experienced.

- Unexpected nature of the death
- Manner of death
- Age of the loved one – young or old
- Depth of your love
- Length of relationship
- Complicated nature of your relationship
- Regrets after the death
- Family dynamics
- Role of faith in your life
- New roles to take on
- Length of their suffering
- Your own ability to process a loss
- Sense of helplessness over the manner of death
- Violent or tragic nature of the death
- Circumstances in your life
- Support system
- Proximity to another loss

How many more can you add? The point is that everything that goes into making you who you are, everything that went into making your loved one who they were, and everything that went into the relationship you had with them *all* affect what your grief journey looks like. Add to that the circumstances surrounding their death and you can see where we're heading.

Is it any wonder that we all have such a unique path? So, does this provide you with a better understanding of why the statement, "I know exactly how you feel" can *never* be true? I hope this gives you a new perspective and some food for thought.

The *only* one who knows exactly how I feel is God. He is the one to whom I run.

"O Lord, you have searched me and known me!
You know when I sit down and when I rise up;
you discern my thoughts from afar."
Psalm 139:1-2

My incredibly gifted graphic designer took my pathetic attempt at illustrating this point visually (which I will *not* be sharing here), and created this beautiful graphic that does an amazing job of showing how so many factors, or "Grief Influencers" alter our grief, for better or for worse. Fill in your own factors.

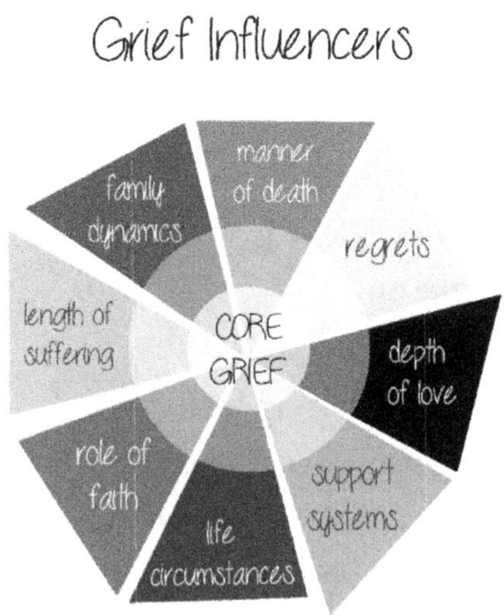

This next post also came from the ministry site, rather than my personal blog, but I think the message fits in here perfectly. Even re-reading it just now, I was reminded how important this concept is.

"The Danger of Comparisons"

Day 820

Do you struggle with making unhealthy comparisons in your life? Let's face it, *seldom* do we feel better after making a comparison to someone else. I've often said that we compare our weaknesses to someone else's strengths. So how could we ever come out feeling better about that?

What's behind this propensity to compare ourselves or our circumstances to others'? When we do try to show ourselves in a better light, those comparisons generally fall into two camps.

1. We want to feel better about ourselves so we look for a comparison that would show us in the best possible light.
2. We are feeling sorry for ourselves and want to throw a pity party. "Nobody knows the troubles I've seen ..." Consequently, we compare our pitiful situation to someone else who clearly doesn't have it as bad as we do.

Anybody relate? I certainly can. Neither one of these scenarios is helpful to either party. But it is the subject of this post.

Before I spend most of the time and space on #2 above, I want to share a few very brief, but true statements about #1. In Psalm 139, we are told that we are "fearfully and wonderfully made." God has designed each of us in his image – and exactly how he intended us to be. Embrace the uniqueness of who you are in Christ and turn those unhealthy comparisons into glorious celebrations!

So as Forrest Gump so eloquently stated, "And that's all I have to say about that!"

Now onto the main purpose for this post – talking about the comparisons we make when we want people to feel sorry for us because nothing could be worse than what we're going through.

More specifically, I'm talking about comparing our losses to someone else's. I've been guilty of it. Because I'm grieving the death of my husband so deeply, I can often feel like few people have hurt as much as I hurt through this. So, I'm speaking these words to myself as much as I am to you, my readers!

Let me throw out some examples of potential comparisons:

- Is it easier if you knew your loved one was dying? Or was it better that you didn't have to watch them suffer?
- Would you rather lose a child at age four, or after you've spent 30 years with them?
- Is it better to lose your spouse when you're young and have a chance at happy times ahead? Or is it better to lose them a few years before *you* die so you'll see them sooner?
- Do you think the loss of your mother is worse than the loss of someone's grandmother who raised them?
- Is it easier to "get over" a loss of a family member that you had a rocky relationship with? (And subsequently deal with hefty guilt?) Or is it better to lose someone you love dearly?
- Should you be grateful you lost your job while you're still young enough to find a new one, or is it easier if you lose it a few years before you planned to retire?
- Is a divorce more or less of a heartache than a death?

Perfect situations to use the phrase I'd like to permanently ban, "Well, at least ... " So, please don't!

I could go on and on ad nauseum with example after example. I could even come up with some *crazy* comparisons. But here's the bottom line. Or more accurately, a couple of bottom lines.

It. Doesn't. Matter! What difference does it make if you think your pain is worse than someone else's? Do you think it lessens theirs because you tell them, "It could be worse. You could be going through what *I'm* going through." Nope. Or do you think it makes *you* feel better because you've just "out-grieved" someone else? Nope again.

There is virtually nothing to be gained by trying to "one-up" someone else who is suffering a loss. This isn't a contest. Nobody wins.

Bottom line #2 – You have no idea what their pain feels like. I've written about this before, but it's worth stressing again. *Everyone's* grief is unique and painful for them at that moment of time, whether they're grieving a job loss or the death of a child. You don't know how they feel, and they don't know how you feel. But all the emotions are valid. End of story.

Over the past two years since Dale's death, as friends have shared with me the heartaches they are dealing with, they often say to me, "I know this isn't as bad as losing a husband." To which I reply, "My pain doesn't lessen yours."

It's absolutely true. Our grief is real and personal and completely independent from what someone else may be suffering through. Don't apologize for grieving. And don't minimize your own pain. Own it. Process it. Cry over it.

And a good reminder for all of us – even if we are suffering, extend compassion and kindness to your friends who are hurting from *anything*. Who better to offer a shoulder on which to cry than someone who understands grieving? Be the unselfish friend they need.

Pray for your hurting friend. And while you're at it, ask God to comfort you in your suffering, too. He understands your pain intimately and his shoulders are big enough for all of us.

"The Lord is near to the brokenhearted
and saves the crushed in spirit."
Psalm 34:8

Forever

Nobody, including me, wants to grieve for the rest of their lives. It's an incredibly difficult place to live and the concept of forever grief is not hopeful. And yet, I believe it deserves some space in this book because it's real and pervasive in the lives of grievers. And I've vowed to be honest with you.

A post I wrote entitled simply "Forever Grief" takes a deeper look at this heartbreaking reality for so many.

"Forever Grief"

Day 683

Do those words strike fear in your heart? Are you tempted to send someone to my house to check up on me? Have I lost my grip on reality? I hope not!

I had the opportunity this past weekend to speak to a group of church volunteers whose ministry is walking alongside those who are hurting, very similar to Stephen Ministers for those familiar with that organization. I am always in awe of those who deliberately choose to step into another person's pain. So, hats off to them and any of you who do that!

I asked the attendees to fill out a comment card after my presentation and one of the questions was, "What most surprised you?" My surprise this time is the number of people who wrote down "forever grief" as their answer.

I do talk about this concept, so let me give you the cliff notes version here and end, as I always strive to, on a hopeful note.

I don't believe *every* thing or person we grieve results in "forever grief." I'm not grieving all the pets I've lost through the years. Nor am I still grieving most/all of my relatives or friends. In fact, while I do certainly miss my parents, I wouldn't even claim that I have a forever grief associated with their losses.

Almost without exception, my memories of these past losses make me smile and feel warm on the inside, despite how deeply I grieved the deaths at the time.

So just what does constitute a "forever grief?" Guess what? *You* get to decide! Yep, no one can tell you what or whom you grieve forever, and what you "should" eventually move on from. Just like grieving in general, forever grief is an incredibly personal thing. No definition. No judgment. Just compassion.

But I'd still like to use a couple of examples to dive into this a little more deeply. Virtually every parent I've talked with who has lost a child experiences forever grief, even if they don't label it as such. In fact, I chatted with a 91-year-old woman this week who lost a daughter decades ago, and yet she still teared up telling me about it.

Friends of mine who have been widows for decades also tell me that it doesn't really get better. While my own widow experience is just under two years old, I can see how the deep love I had for Dale, resulting in the deep grief I feel over his death, could certainly become *my* forever grief.

So based on many conversations I've had and on my own experience, here's the radical statement I want to throw out there. I think sometimes, it's okay to grieve for the rest of your life!

I'm not saying that's *all* you do, but I think we should stop trying so hard just to get past the pain. And stop trying so hard to move others through their pain. That should *not* be our ultimate goal. Because what happens then is this: we stuff the pain down only to have it pop up somewhere down the road in an unhealthy manner.

Achieving a state of no pain and only happiness isn't even biblical. In John 16:33, it says, "In this world you will have trouble, but take heart, I have overcome the world."

We know what happened when Adam and Eve disobeyed God in the Garden of Eden. Sin entered the world and has tainted everything from that point on. Pain and sorrow and death are some of the consequences we suffer because of that.

And as long as we live in this fallen world, we will always have loss and heartache and grieving. And yes, I believe some of it will last forever. So, what do we do with *that*?

First of all, we acknowledge that God does his best and most permanent work through our trials, so we look to see how he wants to deepen our faith and cause us to trust him more. We see *that* for the blessing that it is.

We learn how to live our life despite this trial. We find a new normal. We don't necessarily move on. We don't forget. Perhaps we don't stop grieving. We are now different people because of this loss. On one hand, perhaps forever grieving. But on the other hand, molded by God for his purposes through this pain.

And finally, we look forward to the day when God makes everything right again. Maybe it's when he calls you home. Maybe it's when Jesus returns. But make no mistake, God *will* make it all right. Because, through Jesus' sacrificial death on the cross, he *has* overcome the world. Therein lies our hope. And our joy!

Let that hope and that joy add balance to *your* life that is likely struggling with *something*. Maybe it's minor irritations, maybe it's crises of various types. Perhaps you're in the midst of grieving even now. And maybe you're still suffering through *your* forever grief.

Allow yourself to feel the loss. But always be reminded of God's love for you and for his perfect plan, and let that bring you much joy!

"Count it all joy, my brothers, when you meet
trials of various kinds,for you know that the
testing of your faith produces steadfastness."
James 1:2-3

Exhausting

There's no way around this grief characteristic. I've lost track of the times I've told my friends that I'm exhausted from grieving. The best way to make sense of this is to think about a time when you had a major *mental* task ahead of you. Maybe it was working on your income taxes, or perhaps you had a huge work project that consumed you for weeks. Even managing a busy household can take every ounce of mental capacity you have available.

The point is that your exhaustion likely had nothing to do with physical exertion, with the possible exception of that busy household! Mental exhaustion is equally, or *more* all-encompassing than physical exertion.

Take that level of exhaustion and multiply it by, oh maybe a million! That's how I still feel sometimes, but especially in those early days. Simply put – grieving is hard work! Add to that the fact that our brains are functioning at about 10% capacity and we are just an accident waiting to happen!

As I tried to find medical support for my exhaustion, I penned this blog post for the ministry site that takes a deeper look at the effects on our bodies as we grieve deeply. Not only does this post support the exhaustion theory, but it also looks at the next characteristic.

"What the Long-Term Effects of Chronic Pain Can Teach Us"

Day 673

No, you haven't accidentally landed on the Mayo Clinic website. Although they and many other medical professionals have much to say about this topic.

So, what started me down this particular path? As I near the two-year mark of Dale's death, I was looking for a way to describe the effects of being sad for so long. In a sense, I was trying to explain the phenomenon of second-year widowhood being harder than the first. And as I've heard some widows say, "Years three and four ain't no picnic either!" Great ...

Anyway, as I thought about these past 22 months of emotional pain, I couldn't help but draw the analogy to that of people suffering from chronic *physical* pain. And with my ever-present friend, Google, I unearthed some sobering facts from multiple, well-respected medical sources. Most arrived at remarkably similar conclusions.

The effects of long-term chronic pain read like a medical horror film, both physically and mentally. Here's a sampling of what I found on my search:

- Increased blood pressure
- Increased heart rate
- Reduced ability to fight off illness and disease
- Tense muscles
- Limited ability to move
- Lack of energy
- Change in appetite
- Increased risk of dementia
- Diminished cognitive ability
- Depression
- Anxiety
- Difficulty sleeping
- Anger
- Lack of motivation
- Less interest in rewards

Yikes! Made me send an immediate prayer up to God thanking him for keeping me relatively healthy with little pain. To my friends with chronic pain, I'm so sorry for what you deal with daily. May God give us all a heart of compassion for anyone suffering like this.

So my foray into this medical discovery gave me a bit of a pause. I do believe there is a strong tie between our emotional state and our physical well-being.

However, for me personally, I would *not* go so far as to claim that my long-term *emotional* pain resulted in all those bullet points. But some of those symptoms have certainly been sprinkled, sometimes generously, over these past months since I lost Dale. The good news is that I will *always* take a chocolate reward. (See 'less interest in rewards' above.)

I changed my Google search from "effects of long-term chronic pain" to "effects of long-term grief." I bet you can guess what I found.

Yep – *many* of the same symptoms showed up in both searches. Chronic pain had more physical symptoms and chronic grief more emotional, but the similarities were striking.

My unscientific hypothesis was that long-term grief did, in fact, have many of the same symptoms that long-term physical pain did. It did not take long to reach that conclusion, albeit without any of the necessary regression analyses usually required! (Sorry, the statistician in me snuck out ...)

But in this case, it's not necessary to back up what I found with solid scientific methods. It's enough to see that suffering either physically or mentally can result in additional challenges and risks.

For me, it helps put a bit of a definition on why this second year has been harder – and in many ways doesn't seem to be improving. Simply put – I've been sad for a long time and the cumulative effect is noticeable to me.

If I stopped there, this would be a very pathetic blog post! Hopefully, most of you know me well enough to expect some sort of positive spin on this, right?

This subject easily falls under my teaching of joy and sorrow coexisting in our lives.

Yes, all the above is true for me. The longer I'm without Dale, the sadder and lonelier I am.

But ... I continue to grow in my understanding of how God walks with me, blessing me in ways that I would never experience without this trial. A deep, real-world faith doesn't grow from a bed of roses.

In some ways, it rises from the ashes of our broken lives. But it *does* rise. And therein lies my joy and my hope.

God shows me daily how much he loves me by guiding my steps on this journey, blessing me with friends who still pray for me, giving me a purpose during this season of my life, and reminding me that, in the end, he makes everything right again.

In this quick fix-it world in which we live, please remember that so many people are suffering either physically or mentally or both. Have grace. Be kind. Be patient. Be a blessing.

"Be kind to one another, tenderhearted, forgiving one another, as God in Christ forgave you."
Ephesians 4:32

Relentless

This characteristic isn't significantly different from "exhausting" but my purpose here is to focus on the never-ending nature of grieving. Exhaustion as we discussed above can descend upon the griever on Day One. Relentless, by its very nature, must have some time pass to do its most devastating work.

If we use the "waves" analogy from an earlier chapter, relentless means the waves keep hitting one after another after another with virtually no rest in-between. It can also mean, just when you think you're getting a breather for a spell, here comes another massive wave.

I remember writing this next post and feeling like there was so much randomness to my emotions here. As I look back on this more than a year later, I believe what I was experiencing was this exact characteristic. See what you think.

"The Therapist's Couch"

Day 514

When I began writing this blog over a year ago, the main purpose was to help me process through my grief after losing Dale. It was essentially my therapist's couch! But I was hopeful that I would find little nuggets of wisdom to pass along to the readers as well, so that God could use this blog to help others along their own journey. And honestly, finding that nugget was a goal for each and every post.

Well, today I am deeply entrenched on that therapist couch because today's post is, unfortunately, just me processing some very difficult days. You may get nothing out of this. And for that, I apologize. But I decided last night after another grief-filled day that I needed to pour out my heart, not only to God (as I often do), but to this cyber page.

If you do decide to keep reading, let me preface this with a few disclaimers. This season does *not* mean that my faith in a good God has wavered. I still trust him, still believe in his sovereignty over everything, still turn to him in prayer during my dark moments. And I still cling to his promise of eternal life with him when this life is past – and for my reunion with Dale.

I also still live a pretty normal-looking life on the outside. Most of the time I don't have public breakdowns. I don't walk around with my head down crying, "Woe is me!" I've learned how to function in this new "normal." And yes, that new normal does have times of joy and blessing for which I am truly grateful. Many (most?) people might even think I've healed and moved on. My grieving season must be over.

But the reality is that every single day is overwhelmingly marked by sadness and loneliness. I feel bombarded with memories of my good times with Dale. Not just a couple of times a day, but too many times to even count. I would go so far as to say they are almost a constant presence in my day. It might be a specific memory of something we enjoyed together. But so often, it's the memory of how much I loved him and how much he loved me.

I seem to have no influence over this bombardment. I'm not sitting around for most of the day, trying to conjure up these memories so that I can have a good cry. They can hit me at any time of the day or night – whether I'm sitting quietly or in the middle of an activity with a group of people. Sometimes I know what triggered the memory or the emotion. Other times, they just stab my heart with no warning whatsoever.

It's exhausting. I'm exhausted. I've tried to be a glass-half-full kind of gal most of my life, so it's incomprehensible to me that I've been so sad for 514 days. And to have no idea when the sun will come out again.

You might wonder why those good memories bring me to tears. Clearly, they are bittersweet. I'm grateful beyond words for the life we had together before his dementia stole that from us. But the larger-than-life reality is that those times are over and I long for them ... and him ... like nothing I have ever experienced before. And the depth of the pain and heartache is also like nothing I have ever experienced before.

You might also wonder if there's something fundamentally wrong with me to be grieving this deeply 17 months after his death. Harder now than a year ago. And maybe you silently want me to start taking some meds. I won't rehash my thoughts on that subject here, but feel free to visit a previous post about that!

Over this past year, I have had lots of conversations with other widows or friends who have experienced a deep loss. And either purposefully or accidentally, I've landed on many articles or blog posts written by those suffering a loss.

Almost universally, they talk about how much harder the grieving is two to three years after the loss. Some are still deeply grieving *decades* after the loss. That does not encourage me!

But it does tell me that the reality of this season I'm in is not "just me." I find myself nodding through almost all these articles, relating to their pain and their wonderment at how long it's lasting.

So, no, I don't think the pain I'm still experiencing is unique. What *is* unique is the sharing of it. I believe so many people suffer in silence, not wanting to be an emotional burden on their friends. Or they may share within a grief support group. Those can be extremely healing for anyone grieving a loss, but often the experiences shared there, stay there. And sometimes, just maybe, those experiences need to be shared with the grieving person's circle of support.

Well, I think that's enough gloom and doom for today. Thank you for listening! Since I cried through this whole post-writing, I do feel better! And putting it out there as transparently as I can is healthy and helpful for me.

Do I expect this post to change your interactions with me? Not really. It was never about that. I absolutely understand that people aren't going to be following up with me daily as some did in those early days. And that's how it should be. We do most of the hard work of grieving alone.

So this post is not a call to action for any of you. At the most, maybe it gives you a little perspective. Maybe it busts a myth or two about the length and depth of grieving. Maybe it reminds you to keep praying for me. *That* I will take!

This was just me trying to articulate, mostly for my own benefit, the difficulty of this path I'm on. I will still look for blessings in each day – and I know they will be there. And I will continue to witness God's refinement of me and my faith through this trial.

"The Lord is near to the brokenhearted and saves the crushed in spirit." Psalm 34:18

Confusing

I want to live in a world that makes sense to me. Even though I'm a writer now, I spent most of my career as a numbers person. For goodness sakes, I was a Statistics major! *Nobody* thinks that's any fun. I want two plus two to always equal four. I don't function well when there is a healthy dose of uncertainty in my life.

Truthfully, after Dale died, it didn't matter one iota what I wanted my life to be. This loss and the grief associated with it completely consumed me. And completely stole any illusion of control over my life I thought I had.

So, the only healthy response to that loss of control was to recognize how upside down my life had become and acknowledge that this was my new reality. Fighting against it wasn't going to help. Learning to ride the waves was essential. And hanging onto what *was* certain in my life – my trust in a good God – was more important than ever before. Read on for a few examples of this mixed up life!

"Living with Tension"

Day 291

The title of this post is a bit deceptive, although, not intentionally. I'm not living with tension in the sense that my dogs and cat are fighting all the time. In fact, it's really the exact opposite – they are getting along splendidly, for those of you interested in my canine/feline children.

No, the tension I'm living with is much harder to describe. So maybe I'll just throw some examples out there and let them speak for themselves . The first one I noticed was the tension I felt every evening when I was home. That's when I miss Dale the most and when the loneliness is still sometimes overwhelming, coming in waves. And yet ... I drew comfort from being at home at night, relaxing with a good book or a good TV program, and of course hanging out with Daisy, Winnie, and Max. So, do I fill all my evenings with activities to keep the loneliness at bay? Or do I stay home and avoid any "mom" guilt from leaving my children at home alone again? (And satisfy the homebody part of my personality ...) **Tension #1**

What to do with these tears? On one hand, it's exhausting to cry and grieve the loss of Dale. Honestly, it's still a daily occurrence for me, even though you'd think I'd be about out of tears by now. So that part of me would like to push through this season and reach an equilibrium where I just cry occasionally. And yet ... there's a part of me that almost dreads that day when I don't cry for Dale because I'm afraid it will feel like I don't miss him as much, or love him as much, and I might lose some of my connection to him. My logical mind knows that this makes no sense, but my heart is just not ready to let go of that yet, even though it wants to heal. **Tension #2**

I can feel completely energized by this new ministry to which God has called me – helping others be a blessing to their grieving friends – and sense clear leading from him and a heightened sense of excitement and confirmation as I think through all I've seen from his hand in this part of the journey. When I share what I'm learning with others, either at a presentation or during a one-on-one coffee, I experience a certain level of joy, knowing that I am right where I need to be, in the middle of God's will. And yet ... there's such a large part of me that wants to scream out, "This is *not* the ministry that I want to be in! I want my husband back!" **Tension #3**

This season of grieving can easily draw my attention to the hope of heaven, because I'm tired of hurt and loneliness and sadness. I'm tired of living without Dale. I'm tired of living in a world tainted by sin. I'm tired of seeing how that sin manifests itself in countless ways in this world. It's evident just looking at recent news examples or challenges in the lives of my friends – tornadoes, wildfires, missing college students, chronic illnesses, abuses, cancer diagnoses, addictions, unbelieving children. The list of heartaches goes on and on.

So, I hurt for me, and I hurt for my friends, and I hurt for the world at large. I long for Jesus to return and take his children to heaven where we will spend eternity with him and sing God's praises *forever*! No more pain, no more sorrow, no more tears, no more lonely, no more trials, *no more sins*! It's a beautiful picture and so much of my heart longs for this.

And yet ... Jesus has not returned. I am still here. And so are you. There is still time to be a blessing to others. There's still time to learn more about God and his character. There's still time to let God work in my life, refining me more and more through this trial. There's still time to do his will. There is still time to spread the Gospel message to unbelievers. There's still time to accept God's free gift of salvation through the death of his Son on the cross. Many reasons to long for heaven, and many reasons to keep fighting the good fight. **Tension #4**

Are you starting to get the picture? These are some of the tensions that I live with on a consistent basis. But I don't have a market on this. My guess is that any one of you could create your own list of tensions that may consume your lives. It will be unique to each of you and your personal situation.

What's the lesson in all of this? Not sure I have a clear answer to that, but in part, there is tension built into this world, because ultimately, this is not our home. In Ecclesiastes 3:11, it says, "He has also set eternity in the human heart; ..." So that's part of our issue. We know instinctively that there is more after this life.

I also wonder if perhaps I'm trying too hard to resolve the tensions and find a perfect balance. Lately, I'm beginning to understand that whenever I try to do *anything* in my own strength, it falls short. Is it time to focus on what the psalmist said? "Be still, and know that I am God" (Psalm 46:10). In that stillness, in that quiet, his Spirit can fill us with all that we need.

What's the opposite of tension? How about calmness, contentedness, or peace? That's what I long for, and that's my prayer for you as well.

"May the God of hope fill you with all joy and peace
as you trust in Him, so that you may overflow
with hope by the power of the Holy Spirit."
Romans 15:13

Boy, do you feel like to you need to take a deep breath? Or maybe an ice cream break? I do! Talking through these deep emotions that showcase grief's nature is no easy task. Writing it *or* reading about it may be equally draining, so thank you for hanging in there through this difficult section. There is relief ahead!

And so "the honest griever" digs deep into the realities of grief.

12

Widow Grief

As the author of this book … and a widow, I suppose I have the prerogative to have my very own special chapter! But, all that aside, widow grief is utterly unique and deserves a little extra focus. So, if you are a widow reading this, I hope you'll feel a little less alone – and a little more "justified" in the depth of your heartache when you reach the end of this chapter. If you are a widower reading this book, your grief differs from that of a widow in some aspects, but there are nuggets ahead for you as well.

For any of you who would consider yourselves strictly observers, there is much to be learned, and I thank you for willingly becoming that student.

When Relationships Are Rocky

Before we delve too deeply into "widow grief," I want to acknowledge that many widows or widowers did not have a loving, satisfying relationship with their spouse. Perhaps they grew apart over time, as so often happens, and the love they initially felt for each other deteriorated into a reluctant roommate relationship.

At the other end of that spectrum are the marriages that were filled with all kinds of abuses – physical, sexual, emotional, mental, and even spiritual. I've read many fellow authors' books over the past year or so that catalogued some horrendous abuses, and years of being the only partner truly trying to mend the brokenness.

If this is you, I couldn't be sorrier for the pain and despair and disappointment you endured during your marriage. While mine was not perfect, I always knew I was deeply loved and can't imagine not having that assurance as I grieve this loss.

It's quite likely that many of these chapters thus far didn't resonate exactly with your experience, but this one will unfortunately shine a light more brightly on that disparity. Again, I apologize.

Your less-than-ideal relationship doesn't mean you don't hurt deeply. To a greater or lesser degree, most of us who've lost a spouse grieve the good days we shared. Regardless of how your marriage deteriorated, I suspect you started out deeply in love with high expectations for a long, satisfying relationship. So you grieve on two fronts – one for the good days that are now gone forever, and one for all that you hoped your marriage would be, but wasn't. That's its own special type of grief, too. High expectation and deep disappointment can go hand in hand.

You may also be dealing with friends and family who expect your grief to be less *because* of the condition of your marriage. That can only increase your loneliness because the world around you doesn't allow you to express your deepest emotions. I'm sorry for that pain as well.

Regardless of where your marriage lies on this spectrum, I want us to start together.

God's View of Marriage

The stage is best set by seeing what the Bible says about the special relationship between a husband and a wife. You've probably heard these scriptures often at weddings. They play a huge part in explaining the one-of-a-kind grief that is widow(er)hood.

Let's start with the foundation of marriage as God intended it.

> "He answered, 'Have you not read that he who created them from the beginning made them male and female, and said, "Therefore a man shall leave his father and his mother and hold fast to his wife, and the two shall become one flesh"? So they are no longer two but one flesh. What therefore God has joined together, let not man separate'" (Matthew 19:4-6).

Becoming "one flesh" isn't strictly in the physical sense. A husband and wife make up the unit that most closely reflects the relationship between Christ and the church.

> "'Therefore a man shall leave his father and mother and hold fast to his wife, and the two shall become one

> flesh.' This mystery is profound, and I am saying that it refers to Christ and the church. However, let each one of you love his wife as himself, and let the wife see that she respects her husband" (Ephesians 5:31-33).

In a perfect world, this marriage scenario reflects the powerful relationship that Christ has with the church as a whole. Sin tainted this, too, so none of us has experienced marriage as it was meant to be. But the intent is made clear in these verses.

Several years before my husband died, a friend lost her husband to cancer. One Sunday she was talking with one of the elders in the church about how difficult this loss was for her. His thoughtful – and candid – reply was, "Of course you're hurting. It's like half of your body has been ripped apart."

Yikes! That *does* sound painful, doesn't it? Now that I am in that same boat, I completely get it. I've used that exact description numerous times as I've tried to quantify what this pain is like. So, it should come as no surprise that a blog post showed up dealing with that exact subject! You'll see some recurring themes here.

"No 'Cookie-Cutter' Grief"

Day 466

I lost a good friend to cancer this past week. Her funeral was yesterday and it's still hard to get my head around her absence. She died about a month after receiving the diagnosis. Her friends and family all knew it was terminal and she didn't have a lot of time left. But I think we were all shocked at how quickly it went.

I'm not only grateful for her friendship for the past 22 years, but for the sweet conversations we had over this past month. She lost her beloved husband unexpectedly 15 years ago. I still remember it almost like it was yesterday. And yet for her, I'm sure some of those 15 years dragged painfully on.

But back to those sweet conversations. We spent much of that time talking about what lie ahead for her. Her greatest anticipation was to be with Jesus, in the throne room of God. Because heaven and Jesus are synonymous. You can't have one without the other. That is my ultimate hope as well as I walk through this life. I so look forward to that.

Maybe because we were both widows. Maybe because my loss is much more recent. But we also talked *a lot* about the reunion with her husband. Oh sure, we can often think about how wonderful it will be to reunite with our believing loved ones who have gone on before us. But I think it can often be on a very ethereal level. Somehow, we expect it to be spectacular, but we don't always focus on the reality of it.

Even though I don't *think* my life on this earth will end in a few weeks, I *have* started to contemplate my reunion with Dale in real time, so to speak. I imagine what it would be like to actually wake up in heaven and run into his open arms. And with the Agape love that we would both have? It's mind-blowing to imagine how incredible that will be. That thought sustains me through many lonely days and nights.

So, with my friend's death likely only a few weeks away, I asked her if she could even get her head around what it would be like to be reunited with her husband after all these years. To actually see and touch and hear him again after the loneliness of widowhood. She told me it was surreal to her. Hard to even grasp the reality that was ahead for her.

Honestly? I told her I was a little jealous that she would get to see Dale before I would. I asked her to tell him how much I loved and missed him, and that I couldn't wait for the day we would be reunited as well.

So focused was I on the immeasurable joy that was awaiting my friend, that I found my emotions around her impending death were primarily ... *joyful*! Of course, I would miss her and shed tears over *my* loss. But to a very great degree, that was overshadowed by my incredible happiness for her!

You might suggest that she had the best of both worlds. She knew her time was short, and she made the absolute most of that. She had such precious moments with all her family members and many of her friends. She was able to plan every detail of her "Celebration of Life Service" including asking me to play a piano prelude for it. I was honored to do so. When I asked if she had any specific requests, she said (with a twinkle in her eye), "Something with 'saints' in it!" I loved her sense of humor.

So while she had the opportunity to do all the things we all want to do before we die, she also was blessed to go quickly, without the long, lingering death that so often accompanies cancer. She was ready to go, she knew where she was headed, she and her husband had left a wonderful family legacy, she had lived a good life of service to her Lord, and he blessed her by taking her home quickly.

In the days shortly after she passed, I found myself making some comparisons between her death and Dale's – and more accurately, my response to them.

All the wonderful things that I rejoiced over with my friend were remarkably similar to what Dale has been experiencing for the past year or so. He, too, has now seen Jesus' face. He, too, is in the throne room of God. He, too, has been reunited with his believing family members and friends. They are both experiencing the many promises God has given us in the Bible regarding eternal life. No more sorrow, no more tears, no more sadness.

So, a part of me was wondering why I didn't have the same level of joy after Dale's death. I questioned if my grieving over Dale's death should look more like how I grieved my friend's death. Was I too focused on the pain of his absence from my life, and not enough on all the joy he now had?

I did chew on that for a while and want to share where I landed afterwards.

Of course, there are some obvious differences. For 31 years I lived nearly every day with Dale. I saw my friend regularly, but we weren't part of each other's daily lives. And my love for my friend was that of a sisterhood, while my love for Dale was the earthly version of Agape.

But the biggest, most impactful difference in my response to their deaths is the fact that I had a covenant relationship with Dale. The Bible tells us that when two become one in marriage, it's a relationship that is intended to last "until death do us part." Sadly, I know that isn't true for many, and for those who have experienced that brokenness, I'm sorry for your pain, too.

The loss of a spouse through death is like having half of your body ripped away *because* of that covenant relationship. It's a reflection of the relationship that Christ has with his church, the body of believers. Other than the relationship among the three members of the Trinity, I'm not sure there's a more powerful example than that of husband and wife.

So, it only makes sense that my grieving over Dale's death is on a different level than the grief over my friend's.

And that is *also* a lesson for us. Everyone. Grieves. Differently. A zillion factors can go into that, so be cautious about making assumptions about their grief. Just be that welcome, listening ear when they need to process their unique pain. It's such a precious gift you can give during a vulnerable time. God will bless you in return.

"He will wipe every tear from their eyes.
There will be no more death or mourning or crying or pain,
for the old order of things has passed away."
Revelation 21:4

Widow Grief Touches Everything

Even with the independence we both had in our marriage, I did not feel whole after Dale died. The death of a spouse changes *everything* in your life. Even though Facebook has lots of "issues," I do find parts of that social landscape helpful. Cute dog pix, yummy recipes, and occasionally a post about grief that strikes a chord within me. Such was the case when I found this quote from Kelley Lynn on the "Widows Together" Facebook page.

"The death of a spouse or partner is different than other losses, in the sense that it literally changes every single thing in your world going forward. When your spouse dies, the way you eat changes. The way you watch TV changes. Your friend circle changes (or disappears entirely). Your family dynamic/life changes (or disappears entirely). Your financial status changes. Your job situation changes. It affects your self-worth. Your self-esteem. Your confidence. Your rhythms. The way you breathe. Your mentality. Your brain function. (Ever heard the term 'widow brain?' If you don't know what that is, count yourself as very lucky.) Your physical body. Your hobbies and interests. Your sense of security. Your sense of humor. Your sense of womanhood or manhood. EVERY. SINGLE. THING. CHANGES. You are handed a new life that you never asked for and that you don't particularly want. It is the hardest, most gut-wrenching, horrific, life-altering of things to live with."

Isn't that exhausting to read? Take a moment to let those realities sink in. I can't claim that every piece of that is true for my life, but the vast majority of it is spot-on.

And it didn't even touch on how tasks that used to be shared now fall on the remaining spouse. With the unique nature of everyone's grief, I can't begin to do justice to anyone else's journey. But permit me to speculate for a moment. I'm thinking specifically of the widows and widowers who have had to learn a plethora of new skills, whether it be cooking or shopping, doing laundry or paying the bills, or caring for the yard or car, and on and on.

The new tasks that widows and widowers take on are obviously different in most cases. At the risk of sounding sexist, I'd expect men to *generally* struggle more with household tasks like cooking, cleaning, laundry etc. Women more likely to battle mechanical and possibly automobile or yard issues. Of course, women don't typically have the physical strength of a man, so that affects how we take on certain tasks. While the tasks may vary from men to women, the depth of pain isn't defined by one's gender. We can all suffer greatly from our loss. And taking on roles we never wanted is just one more way.

I also believe our responses to these new roles are often different because of our genders. Again, I'm generalizing, but men may approach this grief from a practical, "fix-it" mentality. How can I take care of this problem? Women, on the other hand, are likely dealing more directly with the emotional impact of the loss. How do I live without this person's love and all they meant to me? Even the ways they try to help their family members and friends through the grief will look different depending on their gender.

There's no end to the ways we can miss our partner, from the practical to the deeply emotional and romantic. "How can I grieve thee? Let me count the ways." Impossible to do, indeed.

This next blog post shines the spotlight on one more way we can miss our loved ones.

"I Lost My Processor!"

Day 479

Don't panic! Don't call the Geek Squad! It's not my computer processor that I've lost. I don't even have one anymore since it's all in my laptop.

No, the processor I'm talking about is my husband. One of the things I'm missing a lot lately is the daily "processing" of our lives together. Most of it was pretty mundane if I think back on it. Just the minutiae of living life with someone for over 35 years.

We were blessed to have a relationship that allowed for discussion on pretty much any topic. So of course, Dale was my "go to" guy no matter what I needed to talk about. And when I shared something I was struggling with, his goal, like most men, was to get it fixed for me. My goal was for him to listen to me and maybe feel just a little sorry for me!

He was the first one I wanted to tell when something wonderful happened in my day. And he would always celebrate and rejoice with me.

I know men say a *lot* fewer words in a day than we women, but I was also Dale's "go to" person when he wanted to share anything good or bad that was going on in his life. It was just part of the rhythm of our lives together.

I miss that ... every day.

Even when he was at the assisted living facility, I still talked to him at least twice a day on the phone, and went to see him almost every day. Yes, the processor was losing a little of its battery, but it was still there.

I think trying to find a new normal in my life has shined a light on this emptiness I'm currently struggling with. Honestly, it's extremely lonely. Yes, I talk to my animals (like Dr. Doolittle ...), but there's not much conversation happening.

I do have friends that I process parts of my life with, sometimes daily, and I'm extremely grateful for that. Recently, one of those friends was on an extended vacation out of the country in a very weird time zone with few opportunities to connect. That was also a very tangible absence.

All of this caused me to take a closer look at what I should be learning through this. I know God works through our trials and I've learned to expect insights from him any time a new heartache finds its way into my life.

I found that the lesson God was teaching me here wasn't a new revelation. He has tried to teach me this before. But, how often does it take multiple knocks on our head to get our attention from God! I'm grateful for his patience.

What he has shown me, once again, is that he is my all-sufficiency. **When I'm sad or lonely or hurting or grieving, my "go to" guy should be God.**

One of my favorite verses is from Philippians 4:6-7 which says, "Do not be anxious about anything, but in everything by prayer and supplication with thanksgiving let your requests be made known to God.

And the peace of God, which surpasses all understanding, will guard your hearts and your minds in Christ Jesus."

There is so much comfort in this verse, and it's a great reminder that we can and should take everything that causes us to be anxious or hurting to the God who knows us better than we know ourselves. He *can* give us that famous "peace that surpasses all understanding."

Yes, he does still bless us with friends and family and church family who can lift us up during our hard times – and they are from him – but I must remind myself that God should be where I want to run *first*.

So, who is your processor? If you're married, it's likely your spouse. Or it might be a parent or child or best friend. Someone in your life helps you work through the good and bad of your days.

Just a couple thoughts to ponder here. As God is trying to teach me, do you find that you go first in prayer to him? Or are you processing everything through an earthly relationship? I have been and continue to be guilty of this, too.

Do you take your processor for granted? It's so easy to do that. I'm sure I did that for most of our married lives. And, let's face it, not every part of our processing is kind and unselfish and patient. Oh no, sometimes processing is just arguing! So, it's hard to always appreciate *those* times.

But I challenge you to look at this part of your life through a lens of gratitude, knowing that someday, you too may lose your processor.

May God always be the one you can count on!

"The Lord is near to the brokenhearted and saves the crushed in spirit."
Psalm 34:18

My Widow World

If I had to use one descriptor to depict what has been true of my life from October 16, 2017 until today, it would be *lonely*. I wish that weren't true. But despite all the other good things that are true in this life of mine, this is still the condition that rises to the top. I constantly tell others how blessed I am to have such great friends. But I have very few family members left, and sadly even those contacts are rare.

Add to that the fact that I work from home and you can see how and why I've landed in this condition. But it's not just me. Widows consistently tell me how lonely they are, even if they have busy lives with children and grandchildren.

I say, "Amen!" to that. The loneliness isn't getting better. I do my best to fill my life with "substitutes," but nothing and nobody will fill the shoes that were left empty when Dale died.

If you can indulge me with one more mostly sad post, I promise we are going to turn a corner soon.

"The Lonely Crowd"

Day 567

Well, isn't that a title that makes you want to jump in and gobble up this post? But it's a subject that's been on my heart for a while now, and one that I believe God has given me some insights to share with you.

First, true confessions. I've been struggling with loneliness *a lot* lately. Not really surprising since the words "lonely" and "widow" are often linked together. Of course, I miss not living my life with Dale – and memories continue to make my heart ache for those bygone days.

A widow friend, whose husband died about eight years ago, told me early on that loneliness was one of the hardest parts of being a widow. And she said she is lonelier now than when he died, because she's been without him longer. Yep, I can certainly relate to that. Getting harder, not easier.

Despite my best efforts to stay active with church and friends and the ministry, the reality is that I spend most of my time alone. Yes, my pets certainly help, but they're no substitute for human interaction. Most of the hard work of grieving is done alone.

Because the circumstances leading to this loneliness aren't going to change, i.e. Dale's *not* coming back, I realize that I am the one who needs to change – or at least figure out how to navigate through this.

This season of loneliness has opened my eyes to a new reality. *Many* people live lonely lives! I'm starting to see this condition in a whole new light. Widows certainly don't have the corner of the market on loneliness. Anyone who is single or divorced or childless must certainly fight these same emotions.

And one doesn't have to *be* alone to be lonely. Many people in unfulfilled relationships suffer as well. Maybe you are an empty-nester and your loneliness is a result of a quiet house now that the kids are gone.

I just did a quick Google search on "the loneliness crisis" and was shocked at how many articles address this subject. Multiple studies suggest that up to half of their respondents describe themselves as lonely. Loneliness has been called an epidemic and a public health crisis more serious than obesity.

Of course, everyone has an opinion on what's behind this crisis, from sleep deprivation to social media to prescription drugs. There's no shortage of opinions on the causes or the solutions.

But for the believer, that solution list might look a bit different. As I've prayed over this and studied the scriptures, here are some of the insights God has graciously given to me.

- **My loneliness is not unique.** Even Jesus knew loneliness, and certainly never more than as he was dying on the cross. David wrote endless passages in the Psalms about his times of loneliness. So to a certain degree, it *is* one of the sorrows we will suffer in this lifetime. And there is comfort in knowing that our Savior experienced a loneliness greater than we can imagine. He understands this pain.
- **Focus on eternity.** I find great comfort in thinking about spending eternity with Jesus and my loved ones in heaven. Meditating on God's promises of no more tears, no more sadness, no more sorrow, no more *loneliness*, is a great balm for my soul!
- **Be grateful for times of fellowship.** I want to appreciate more and more the time I spend with good friends. We were not created to live in isolation. God wants us living in fellowship with others, and I want to soak up that joy and preserve it for as long as I can. Maybe even take a portion of it into my lonely days and nights.
- **Deepen my relationship with God.** There's no better time for this than when a heart is hurting and longing for relief. God's Word is full of promises to bring joy and peace to your soul. In fact, just this morning as I was contemplating this blog topic, God brought this scripture to my mind: "I have loved you with an everlasting love" (Jeremiah 31:3). Boy, it doesn't get any

better than that! Lord, help me to run to you for comfort in my loneliness.

- **Learn to rest in God alone.** I know this is similar to the previous point, but I want to stress that sometimes we need to learn contentment in our loneliness. Be careful what you use to fill up your lonely life, or substitute as a temporary fix. God is all-sufficient.
- **Do something for others.** This is good advice for anyone at any time. Pouring ourselves into someone else's life, especially someone who is hurting, shifts the focus from our pain to their comfort. I know it's so hard to get started on this one, but the rewards are many.

So, if you are one of the many who struggles with loneliness, you are not alone! That knowledge, however, is generally not enough to make any of us feel any better. Know that Jesus is our forever friend, one who sticks closer than a brother. He will never leave us or forsake us. Pour out your heart to him, and then let him pour his love back into you.

"Draw near to God and he will draw near to you."
James 4:8

Just as in the previous chapter, this is not an exhaustive discussion on the mysteries of widow(er)hood. But I am hopeful that it provided either comfort in the "misery loves company" fashion for those of you suffering the loss of a spouse. Or, for those of you dealing with other kinds of heartache, perhaps there were still some nuggets to help you through your specific pain.

And so "the honest griever" experiences heartache unlike anything she's suffered in her life.

13

Why Grieving?

Not to be confused with the subject of the first chapter in this section – "Why Grief?" – I want to look at the *importance* of grieving in this chapter. And delve deeper into the risk we run of further emotional damage if we deny ourselves the process of working through this grief.

Most of this book thus far has assumed that the grieving process has begun. Since I'm writing primarily from my own experience, it reflects the fact that I jumped into the work of grieving simultaneously with Dale's death. Maybe it's because I was already grieving much of what we lost long before he died. But I didn't go through a long period of denial. I was fully aware of what had happened and, although I deeply dreaded it, I knew I had to deal with it head on.

Again ... It's Unique

So first a few reminders of this unique process:

- The onset of the grieving process *and* the path it takes are both highly individualized. Some may jump immediately into full acknowledgement of the loss, as I did. Others may take years before finally addressing their loss.
- There isn't one right way to approach this. Some may talk to a pastor or counselor. Others will process it with their family members. Friends may play a pivotal role in working through the loss. Praying to God and asking for his help is crucial for many of us. Some, like myself, may find great benefit by writing through their grief, whether it be journaling, blogging, or book writing.

- Grieving is *not* a sign of weakness.
- All the nuances of this journey that we outlined in Chapter 11 and illustrated with the "Grief Influencers" graphic affect how and when the grieving begins in earnest.
- Do you have obligations that you must step back into immediately? Or does your lifestyle allow time for reflection?
- Are you surrounded by family members, or will you be grieving at home alone?

All these circumstances and many more will affect how quickly and completely you immerse yourself in the hard work ahead. So I can't give you a template for what will work best for you.

Risks of Ignoring Your Pain

One thing I do know; if you stuff this pain down, if you deny that you are hurting, if you force yourself to always hold it together, if you don't cry, if you *never* acknowledge the devastating blow you've been dealt, it will damage you physically, emotionally, and spiritually for the rest of your life.

Not only will your own health be compromised in so many ways, but relationships with your family and friends will also likely suffer. And maybe most importantly, you will have missed the invaluable opportunity to run to God with your pain, and experience *his* healing power. So much of what I chronicle in the next section only happened *because* I turned to God during my darkest days.

Keeping all your emotions wrapped up inside will rob you of the joy awaiting you when you let God be your comforter. You will miss living out the reality of all the promises in the Bible related to the Great Healer. *This life* is when we can walk through our valleys with God. Don't waste the opportunity. Let him bring beauty into your life from the ashes of your heartache.

Proof that God is the Great Comforter

Living out these biblical promises from God on my grief journey was one of the most powerful forces in my healing process. I want to pass along as much of my enlightenment as possible and space doesn't allow me to do that justice here. So I've written a 14-day devotional that looks at how we can best walk with God through any season of our life. It is a free download for you at the end of the book. I hope and pray it brings you to God like a hurting child runs to his parent.

Is there biblical support for grieving? Absolutely! There would be no need for *comfort* throughout the Bible if there wasn't grief and heartache preceding it.

So I did a little word search to help illustrate this point. Of course, this isn't the definitive study on this subject because context plays a vital role in each of these texts. But it does give us a sense of the importance of mourning – and receiving comfort in that suffering.

Here are the results, using the New International Version and the Bible-Gateway.com website.

Word	Word Count
• Compassion	82
• Comfort	71
• Grief/Grieve	62
• Tears	42
• Weep/Weeping	150
• Mourn	137

That is a significant representation and confirms not only the expectation of grieving, but the accompanying comfort provided throughout the scriptures.

Here are just a few favorite texts I continue to find comfort through.

> "Blessed be the God and Father of our Lord Jesus Christ, the Father of mercies and God of all comfort, who comforts us in all our affliction so that we will be able to comfort those who are in any affliction with the comfort with which we ourselves are comforted by God" (2 Corinthians 1:3-4).

> "Do not fear, for I am with you; Do not anxiously look about you, for I am your God. I will strengthen you, surely I will help you, surely I will uphold you with my righteous right hand" (Isaiah 41:10).

> "Even though I walk through the valley of the shadow of death, I fear no evil, for you are with me; your rod and your staff, they comfort me" (Psalm 23:4).

> "The LORD is near to the brokenhearted and saves those who are crushed in spirit" (Psalm 34:18).

> "Trust in the LORD with all your heart and do not lean on your own understanding. In all your ways acknowledge him, and he will make your paths straight" (Proverbs 3:5-6).

> "Blessed are those who mourn, for they shall be comforted" (Matthew 5:4).

"When you pass through the waters, I will be with you;
and through the rivers, they shall not overwhelm you;
when you walk through fire you shall not be burned,
and the flame shall not consume you" (Isaiah 43:2).

"You have kept count of my tossings; put my tears in your bottle. Are they not in your book?" (Psalm 56:8).

"Father of the fatherless and protector of widows
is God in his holy habitation" (Psalm 68:5).

I could go on and on, but I think you get the point. The Bible is *full* of examples of grieving and comfort. Why would we think that the God who inspired these scriptures, and who created us in his image, would expect anything less from us. Grieve and experience godly comfort.

Tears

One more point I'd like to make which is both scientific and spiritual. (I happen to believe they don't have to be contradictory, but that's not a subject for this book!)

The subject is tears. You see from the word search that tears and weep appeared almost 200 times in the texts. That's not insignificant! So, first the science behind it.

In some of my ministry research, I found numerous scientific articles that looked at tears. When scientists compared the physiological make-up of onion-peeling tears to emotional tears, they were different! There are toxins in the emotional tears that were absent in the others. Our body has been designed to heal through our tears. Isn't that an amazing fact? And more specifically, *God* has *created* us to heal through our tears. Who can argue with the science *and* the scriptures?

I'd like to end with a blog post that looks at another misconception about grieving.

"Strong Enough to Grieve"

Day 648

That's kind of a strange title, isn't it? It's been rumbling around in my head for the past few days, so I decided to see where this goes.

At the heart of this issue is the question, "Do 'strong' people grieve less than 'weak' ones?" A few months after Dale's death, a good widow friend called me. Honestly, I thought I would have heard from her much sooner than that. When I gently brought that up, she said to me, "I just thought you were so strong." To which I replied, "No one is strong enough to lose the love of their life and not grieve."

That's the short answer, but let's dig a little deeper into this concept.

Anyone who's known me for any length of time may consider me a strong person. I've been self-sufficient for much of my life, even though Dale's strength always undergirded our marriage. I had a career that required me to be business savvy and tough. I was the sole caregiver to four people over the course of 20 years, including my husband. All things that require a certain level of strength.

But that's not always a good thing. Case in point - when Dale asked my dad if he could have my hand in marriage, my dad seriously cautioned Dale because he thought I was a bit too headstrong! Dale said he was up to the task, and he surely was. That conversation still makes me smile.

And yet, 21 months after losing Dale, I don't feel that I have exhibited any strength in this journey. I'm sad daily. I still cry over so many memories. I constantly ask God to give me *his* strength. Sometimes I can't even attend events because it's hard to be around families and couples when I must go alone. I could go on and on with examples.

So, I process all of this through this blog, through the blog on my ministry site, through speaking engagements, and book and song writing. They are the outlets for my pain. God has given me this ministry to share my journey and what he's teaching me with all of you.

I doubt if any of my posts would paint me as strong during this season. Becoming a widow has shone a light on how much I rely on God's strength to get me from one day to the next. None of my own strength has been sufficient.

As I write, I often find other widows or people suffering from losses who comment that it helps them to know what I struggle with because it's their struggle, too. Or, maybe they had some of the same hurts as mine, but didn't know how to tell anyone. So they suffered alone or in silence. Maybe they were afraid they'd be considered weak.

So I write for all of us who are suffering – especially those who don't feel equipped to share their pain. I don't think that makes me strong. I think it makes me honest, and often vulnerable. But if it helps shed some light on these difficult days, then I'm grateful God has called me to this.

Back to the original question. So while it might seem logical that "strong" people don't grieve as deeply, the reality is that no amount of our own strength is enough to get through a deep loss.

Worth repeating - for me, this loss just shines a light on my need for God and his strength. The only "strong" thing I do is face my grief. Thanks for listening.

"My grace is sufficient for you, for my power is made perfect in weakness." Therefore, I will boast all the more gladly of my weaknesses, so that the power of Christ may rest upon me.
2 Corinthians 12:9

This has been a rough section, hasn't it? But its inclusion in this book and "magnifying glass" approach were essential to live up to the title of "honest griever." The heartache is front and center in this journey and looking at it from all angles was a necessary evil, of sorts.

I commend you for hanging in there with me thus far! I'm sure it wasn't always easy reading. I guarantee it wasn't easy writing!

But I've been promising better days ahead and I can finally deliver that for you. Turn the page as we turn the corner and look for that light through this darkness.

And so "the honest griever" finds her own unique way of processing her heartache.

SECTION IV

Silver Linings

We can now *finally* come out of the darkness and into the light! I can't help but start singing the song from *The Wizard of Oz* when Dorothy, Toto, and her motley crew of misfits finally come through the forest and see the Emerald City.

But in our case, we're stepping into the *Son*, and into *his* Light. My apologies for getting that song stuck in your head!

The phrase "silver lining" always has a positive connotation to it and speaks to how even the most difficult of situations can have some good in them. And to a degree, that's what I want this to represent. Even through the heartbreaking loss of my husband, I saw blessings nearly every day.

The other assumption made about silver linings is that most of the clouds are dark and foreboding, with just a lovely sliver of silver. While I acknowledge that many of my days felt just like that, the reality is that, in the scope of eternity and all of God's goodness, all I really had was a dark lining well hidden by glorious white fluffy clouds!

I'm confident that when I reach heaven, the difficult days of this season of my life will not be visible in retrospect. I also expect that ten years from now, even though I will still grieve this loss, I will more and more clearly see the silver and *gold* in the lining from God.

This is a *hopeful* section. We'll look more closely at God's character and his promises. I examine the amazing ways that God works *through* our trials. The last two chapters will be full of blog posts as I show you the times God opened my eyes to new understanding of scriptures and share story after story where I clearly saw God moving as only he can. Happier days are ahead!

14

God's Character and Promises

Much like the chapter where we examined the nature of grief, where I could only scratch the surface of its characteristics, this chapter faces the same challenge. Volumes have been written on God's character and promises, with the most notable being the Bible, God's Word to his people.

So, this meager attempt at exploring this Almighty God will simply be a list of what I found most dear to me – and what I clung to most tightly through this grueling journey. I hope it's a list that is helpful for you as well, or causes you to make your *own* list of favorite "God qualities."

GOD'S CHARACTER

All-Sufficient

You probably saw this characteristic pop up in several of the earlier blog posts I shared. I list this characteristic first because it was where I needed to land time after time. When others failed me, when I had no strength of my own, when I knew no one could understand my pain – I was reminded that God was my all-sufficiency.

Webster's dictionary includes a definition of "All-Sufficiency" as, guess what? **GOD**! Yep, even in this secular world, God is, literally, the very definition of all-sufficiency. He is infinitely able to provide all that we could need or want, within his will for our lives.

I was reminded of this truth daily and often, it seemed, after I had tried everything else to ease my pain or my loneliness. Hit me over the head again, God! He patiently reminded me, after all the times I tried to replace him with other means, that he is and will always be my all-sufficiency. I long for him to always be the first place I run. Is he your "go-to" God?

Empathetic

As alluded to above, God was the only one who could truly empathize with my heartache. That doesn't mean many friends weren't incredible comforters to me. They absolutely were. They helped me through long, dark days with sympathetic *or* empathetic hearts. I am eternally grateful to them.

But God is the only one who knew *exactly* what I was going through. To delve deeper into that thought, I want to examine it from the perspective of the Trinity – Father, Son and Holy Spirit. As the hymn "Holy, Holy, Holy" so beautifully and simply explains, "God in three-Persons, blessed Trinity." The three members of this Godhead are all equally divine, and each have special roles within it. Let me illustrate by looking briefly at the role I saw each take in comforting me.

God, the Father – God is the Creator of the universe and he created *me*. Who could know me more intimately than my Creator? Psalm 139:13-14a looks at this relationship – "For you formed my inward parts; you knitted me together in my mother's womb. I praise you, for I am fearfully and wonderfully made." That entire Psalm is a wonderful reminder of how intimately God knows and understands us. He's been with me since before I was born. This is true for all of you, as well. You are uniquely created and deeply known and loved by Almighty God. What a thought!

Jesus, the Son - While Jesus walked this earth, he experienced incredible temptations and suffering. In Hebrews 4:15, we read, "For we do not have a high priest [Jesus] who is unable to sympathize with our weaknesses, but one who in every respect has been tempted as we are, yet without sin." So, firstly, he experienced the full weight of what it means to be human (while remaining simultaneously divine), and yet he did not sin.

Unlike other world religions, Christianity has a *suffering Savior*. Jesus experienced the most horrific scourging and death on the cross, paying the penalty for our sins. As I've read accounts of what Jesus would have endured, it always brings me to tears as I try to imagine how excruciating his death must have been. But even more horrendous than the physical death, was the fact that God himself turned away from Jesus as he bore that penalty. Separation from his Father is unimaginable.

All that to make the point that Jesus absolutely understands suffering – both physical and spiritual. So when I need someone who truly gets it when I'm missing my husband, Jesus fills that need. This suffering Savior can speak directly into your pain, too. Allow him to be that for you.

The Holy Spirit – This member of the Trinity is often the most difficult to understand, but the role of the Spirit is crucial. When we become believers, it's *this* Spirit that comes to live inside us, guiding us and comforting us as no one else can. And his power is infinite. A few scripture texts will provide a much better explanation than I can.

> "If the Spirit of him who raised Jesus from the dead dwells in you, he who raised Christ Jesus from the dead will also give life to your mortal bodies through his Spirit who dwells in you" (Romans 8:11).

The same power that raised Jesus from the dead is living inside of us as believers. You can't get any closer, or more powerful than that!

> "Likewise the Spirit helps us in our weakness. For we do not know what to pray for as we ought, but the Spirit himself intercedes for us with groanings too deep for words. And he who searches hearts knows what is the mind of the Spirit, because the Spirit intercedes for the saints according to the will of God" (Romans 8:26-27).

So, when I have no words to speak, the Holy Spirit speaks for me directly to God. Many times all I truly had were "groanings too deep for words." Does that give you comfort? Knowing that God's Spirit can intercede for you when words fail you? It's an overwhelming, but comforting reality.

What a powerful team of empathizers I had working on my behalf! I never felt the need to explain to God how I was feeling. It was an incredible relief knowing he was intimately aware of my needs, without me uttering a single word. I pray that you, too, may find this same comfort during your dark days.

Sovereign

Ah, my favorite characteristic of God! No matter what happens or when or how, I know that God is in control of every aspect of my life and will work good through these circumstances. I take a more extensive look at how God works through our trials as the subject of the next chapter. But as *my* favorite characteristic, I couldn't let this chapter go by without an honorable mention!

Fruits of the Spirit

I'm going to kill a lot of birds with this one stone. That same Spirit that we just explored a few paragraphs earlier, has a laundry list of wonderful characteristics. "But the fruit of the Spirit is love, joy, peace, patience, kindness, goodness, faithfulness, gentleness, self-control; against such things there is no law" (Galatians 5:22-23).

Not only do these characteristics describe God's Spirit, but they are also all available to us as believers So, when I needed to feel joy or peace or patience, I need not look any further than within myself, thanks to the Holy Spirit.

GOD'S PROMISES

I know of no better way to describe the promises from God that continue to sustain me on this journey than to simply list them. These are just a few of the ones I went back to again and again.

> "It is the Lord who goes before you. He will be with you; he will not leave you or forsake you. Do not fear or be dismayed" (Deuteronomy 31:8).

> "When you pass through the waters, I will be with you; and through the rivers, they shall not overwhelm you; when you walk through fire you shall not be burned, and the flame shall not consume you" (Isaiah 43:2).

> "Blessed be the God and Father of our Lord Jesus Christ, the Father of mercies and God of all comfort, who comforts us in all our affliction, so that we may be able to comfort those who are in any affliction, with the comfort with which we ourselves are comforted by God" (2 Corinthians 1:3-4).

> "Come to me, all who labor and are heavy laden, and I will give you rest" (Matthew 11:28).

> "I have said these things to you, that in me you may have peace. In the world you will have tribulation. But take heart; I have overcome the world" (John 16:33).

> "Even though I walk through the valley of the shadow of death, I will fear no evil, for you are with me; your rod and your staff, they comfort me" (Psalm 23:4).

"Peace I leave with you; my peace I give to you. Not as the world gives do I give to you. Let not your hearts be troubled, neither let them be afraid" (John 14:27).

"For this light momentary affliction is preparing for us an eternal weight of glory beyond all comparison" (2 Corinthians 4:17).

"The Lord is near to the brokenhearted and saves the crushed in spirit" (Psalm 34:18).

"May the God of hope fill you with all joy and peace in believing, so that by the power of the Holy Spirit you may abound in hope" (Romans 15:13).

"Father of the fatherless and protector of widows is God in his holy habitation" (Psalm 68:5).

"Fear not, for I am with you; be not dismayed, for I am your God; I will strengthen you, I will help you, I will uphold you with my righteous right hand" (Isaiah 41:10).

"He sets on high those who are lowly, and those who mourn are lifted to safety" (Job 5:11).

"For I consider that the sufferings of this present time are not worth comparing with the glory that is to be revealed to us" (Romans 8:18).

God's Word is chock-full of comforting verses like these. As much as I found them individually helpful and encouraging, there's something about seeing them all in totality. Like a balm washing over my soul as I read through them back to back. I hope it felt like that to you as well. Or maybe you create your own list. There are enough verses for everyone!

And so "the honest griever" remembers the God whose promises never fail.

15

God Works through Our Trials

"Being left alone by Satan is not evidence of being blessed." This quote closed out one of my recent daily devotionals from *Streams in the Desert* (Zondervan, rev. 1999). I'd love to give credit to the coiner of this phrase, but there was no name attached to it. But I thought it was too good *not* to use for this chapter.

Lots of hard truths in that short phrase. Do you agree or disagree with the statement? I've done both through the years. As I've said before, I was blessed with an idyllic life for most of my years. While I certainly had the typical frustrations and losses in my life, they were far outweighed by the blessings.

Hanging onto the Good Life

I clearly remember a time about 13 years ago when Dale and I had just returned from an amazing trip to Hawaii, celebrating a couple of big birthdays and our twentieth wedding anniversary. One of my part-time jobs back then was working at a dog kennel. I was in the play yard with a few pooches and telling God how grateful I was for the life I was living. I went on to tell him how blessed I was in virtually every area of my life.

I had a wonderful life growing up, mostly fun college years, challenging but rewarding corporate career, incredible husband and marriage, great friends, beautiful acreages on which to live, supportive and God-centered church family, and my health. Because, as we all know, if you've got your health, you've got everything! So the saying goes. But for me, the real topper to it all was my gratitude for my salvation. That was at the heart of my thankfulness and all the rest was just icing on the cake.

Part of my "strategy" with God was to make sure he knew how much I appreciated everything in my life, so that he wouldn't take it away. Pretty sure God can't be "handled!"

"If God Is Good ..."

About this same time, I was reading the aforementioned book by Randy Alcorn, *If God is Good; Faith in the Midst of Suffering and Evil* (Multnomah, 2014). This was *not* an easy book to read for a variety of reasons. The theology was deep and often required several times through the paragraphs to grasp what the author was teaching. The examples he used throughout the book of people going through horrendous difficulties were painful to read. From my earlier blog post, here's a recap of how many of Alcorn's examples experienced their trials.

> *The author cited story after heartbreaking story of people and couples and families who had been through tremendous difficulties in their lives (or were still in them) – and were often very angry with God or whomever they could blame for the tragedy at the time. And yet, in retrospect, many of these stories ended with those involved being grateful for the lessons they learned, for the deepening of their faith, for the way they saw God using their tragedy to help others. They would even go so far as to say that, despite the horrific experience they went through, they wouldn't trade it for all that they've gained in their knowledge and relationship with God because of it.*

Now I realize not everyone who suffers through a trial comes out sunny side up. I've known people whose lives have been decimated by the tragedies they've suffered, and they never experienced those glorious revelations of how God refined them. I can't speak to why some people never experience ultimate growth from their trial. I'm sure the reasons are as varied as the circumstances. But I *can* speak from my own experience as to how heartbreak can be used to mold us into examples that God will use for his glory. And I will speak to that in a moment.

But first, back to the rest of the story from Mr. Alcorn's book. After the grueling process of working through this deep, reflective book, I felt ... left out. Yep. The contrast between my mostly blessed life and the tragic lives of the examples in the book was stark. Time after time, Alcorn's guests in his book share, in their own words, every heart-wrenching detail of their trials and then the awe-inspiring personal and spiritual growth that emerged as they recognized God working through their trials.

The sheer volume of these stories was staggering. Every kind of devastation you can imagine was showcased and the stories of recovery were unbelievable. I was deeply moved to read their testimonies as they gave God the credit for molding them into the people they had become. And yes, I wanted what they had. Why hadn't God tested me like he did all these people? Did he think I wasn't strong enough to endure the fire of refinement?

I had no answers to those questions at that point in my life. And quite frankly, I moved on. I didn't think about it as I continued with my happy life. Fast forward about six years and Dale's dementia and physical decline have now forced us to move out of that idyllic life in the country, and into town and into a year of tragedies. Fast forward four more years and I am now a widow.

Guess what? I didn't feel left out anymore! This was now *my* time to experience hardship and allow God to work in my life so that the person I had become could ultimately give the glory back to him. But, make no mistake, it was a deliberate decision on my part, albeit an often very reluctant one. It did not happen naturally, due in part to my sinful and stubborn nature. But ultimately, I wanted God to use my pain for eventual good. Of course, I still grieved deeply – even today – but my focus is on allowing God to use me as an example to those around me.

The story of Joseph in the Old Testament is one of my favorites. He suffered one injustice after another. It often seemed as though God had forgotten him. But through unjust accusations and imprisonments, Joseph eventually was released and rose to be second in command to Pharaoh. Ultimately, his position allowed him to save his father and brothers (who originally sold him into slavery) when they came to Egypt during the famine looking for food.

Eventually, Joseph reveals his true identity to his family and there is a tearful reunion. The verse that summarizes so beautifully this entire episode is from Genesis 50:20, "As for you, you meant evil against me, but God meant it for good, to bring it about that many people should be kept alive, as they are today." It's also a verse that I cling to whenever I'm weighed down by troubles in my life. I pray it can be that for you as well.

Back to Alcorn's book; coincidentally, I did read it again after Dale's death and found myself squarely in the club with those saints I had admired years before. Now I just had to finish well, as they did.

Where do you find yourself on your journey through pain? Are you expecting God to use that pain to mold you into a more Christ-like person? What do you want others to see when they look at your life during this difficult season? I want them to be amazed at the God who walks me through this.

How I Found Purpose in My Pain

What does "finishing well" look like? What pieces must be in place for this pain to end in greater purpose? How would my thinking need to change? And what part of myself would I need to give up to God?

I believe certain building blocks had to be in place before this magical transformation would take place. And not surprisingly, it came back to some of the same characteristics of God that we just discussed in the previous chapter.

This is what I had to believe at the outset of this journey:

- God is sovereign over all that happens in my life.
- God has had a plan for this season in my life since before I was born.
- God *will* work good through this heartache.
- God is trustworthy.
- God will never leave me.
- God will walk every step of this journey with me.

These were the foundations *mostly* in place as I stepped into this scary unknown. I didn't nail it 100% of the time and God often had to remind me of these truths. Sometimes I couldn't see through my tears. Sometimes I didn't want to let go of the control. Sometimes I just wanted to have a pity party.

But God is a patient, loving Father, who wholly understands our weaknesses. Every time I lost sight of these building blocks, he would remind me, sometimes gently, sometimes with a knock to the head! Eventually he got my attention. This isn't a one-and-done lesson. Like so much of what we learn about God, it takes repetition for it to sink into our souls.

What if you're currently struggling through a loss of your own, but those building blocks aren't there for you? Maybe your life's journey hasn't caused those truths to be established in your life. To that I would say, "There's no time like the present!"

Ask God to give you the assurance of these truths. Search the scriptures for texts that affirm these over and over again. Find someone who can explain these truths to you. I end this chapter with a long list of scriptures about how God works through our trials, so find those that speak to your heart. Then believe that God loves you and wants you to put your faith in him as he walks with you, or carries you, through this trial.

In the blog post entitled "Reflections on the Six-Month Anniversary," I wrote about how I was beginning to see this growth process start, and I was in awe of it. I felt then as I do now; God does his best and most permanent work in our lives through trials.

As complicated as the concept can be, there are some simple statements that attempt to capture it. Permit me to repeat a few of them from that post.

- *How could I see the Light if I weren't in the darkness?*
- *How much more clearly do I see God and his love for me once all of the peripheral "clutter" of life is stripped away?*
- *How could I so look forward to an eternity with Christ and no more suffering if I hadn't suffered here on earth?*
- *How could I clearly hear God's voice if I weren't forced to sit quietly and listen for it?*
- *How would I know if my God-given faith could stand this test if I wasn't asked to trust it alone?*

Your trial and mine are the fertile soil in which our faith and our understanding of God can grow and flourish. God supplies the sunshine and the rain – so long as we don't put our umbrella of self-control or self-pity up and block out those essential elements!

Nature Reveals Struggles

Speaking of nature, have you ever stopped to think about all the ways God's creation reflects the reality of "growth through adversity?" Once you recognize this concept woven into the fabric of the universe, you can start to develop a greater appreciation of its validity.

Here are just a few examples that illustrate this truth:

- The emperor moth must struggle to break free from the cocoon that has encased it during its infancy *so that* its wings become strong enough to allow it to soar. Man's attempt at "freeing" the poor thing by widening the cocoon opening results in … death.
- When the eagle wants to rise above a storm quickly, it uses the raging storm to lift it above the clouds. This eventually gives the eagle an opportunity to glide and rest its wings. It *uses* the storm to reach calmer skies.
- Any good gardener knows that one of the best ways to coax additional growth from plants is to prune them. Take out the dead unproductive parts. The result is more fruit, more growth, more production. More of what the plant was intended for.

- The devastation of raging storms such as hurricanes, tornadoes or even wildfires can quickly be replaced by fresh new growth. That destruction often results in a new beginning.
- Some scientists believe that strong winds help a tree's roots grow deeper into the earth, allowing it to weather the next storm more effectively.
- In a similar manner, strong winds, in conjunction with a tree's ability to *sway* with that wind, create a stronger trunk system.
- The trees that are *most* protected in a forest are often the weakest.

The correlation between struggling and growth is unmistakable in God's nature. Why should we be surprised that he uses this same concept to help us attain incredible growth?

I want to share a blog post I wrote right after the six-month reflections post. It speaks to how this principle we've been discussing is applicable to a whole host of trial-types.

"Your Turn"

Day 192

After my last blog post, I received responses from several friends letting me know that they were going to start applying the principles I shared about God working best through our trials to whatever trial they were going through.

And that got me thinking - it's such an important lesson that I just might stretch it out into a second blog post. But this time, I don't want to talk about what I'm going through. I want to shine the spotlight on all the myriad ways that people go through trials and suffering and hopefully reveal that *my* lesson can be *your* lesson.

To recap, I shared how God is clearly refining me through my fire of losing Dale six months ago. But how many other struggles are people going through right now? How about just in the lives of those of you reading this blog?

Some have also lost a spouse and are grieving that deeply. Others have lost parents, children, siblings, other relatives, friends, neighbors, even pets. Who or what you grieve doesn't conform to a pre-approved list.

What about the other ways you are grieving? What about that broken relationship with a family member? Or a friend? Or that issue with an addiction that either you or a loved one is struggling with? Or the news that someone dear to you has cancer? Or someone dear *continues* to fight cancer? Or what about your own physical or mental health challenges that don't have answers – or healing? What about a marriage that is struggling? What about a job that is challenging, or boring, or too stressful? What about dreams unfulfilled? I think you get the idea. I could go on and on ...

Recently I had lunch with a friend and we were discussing this exact topic. I said to her, "This world is not short on ways that people grieve." And she wisely answered, "No, but it is short." In other words, this world in which we live, that often can seem to be endless, particularly during trials, is really just a whisper in time. James 4:14 says, "What is your life? For you are a mist that appears for a little time and then vanishes." For Christ-followers, the exceptional news is that eternity with Jesus is what awaits after this mist is gone!

A few weeks ago, I was blessed to have tickets to the MercyMe concert at Wells Fargo Arena in Des Moines. Probably one of, if not the best concert I have ever attended. They performed one of my favorite songs, "Even If," and Bart Millard, the songwriter and lead singer, shared the story behind this song. He has a 16-year-old son who has had diabetes since he was two years old. And of course, Bart has been praying for healing for 14 years, and seeing his son suffer with this disease just breaks this father's heart.

He referred us to the story from Daniel 3 about the three men (Shadrack, Meshack, and Abednego) who would *not* bow down and worship the golden image as King Nebuchadnezzar had commanded everyone to do. And if anyone refused, they would be thrown into the fiery furnace. These godly men told the king, "Our God whom we serve is able to deliver us from the burning fiery furnace, and he will deliver us out of your hand, O king. **But if not**, be it known to you, O king, that we will not serve your gods or worship the golden image that you have set up" (emphasis mine).

Well, if you remember any of your stories from Sunday School days, you know that the furnace did not kill them or hurt them. In fact, there was not even the smell of fire on these men. If you're interested in the whole story, you can read it in Daniel 3:8-30.

The men trusted that God would protect them, but the lesson that Bart Millard learned from this passage is that even if God wouldn't protect them, they would never have bowed down to the golden image. Hence was born the powerful song "Even If."

So, let's get back to the main message of this post – how God refines us through our own fires. For those of us grieving the physical loss of a loved one, we know that God is not likely to bring them back from the dead, even though he is powerful enough to do so.

But what about all those other sorrows you're grieving? Couldn't God restore your broken relationships? Couldn't he heal your cancer, or your loved one's? Just reread that earlier paragraph with the myriad of heartaches. Yes, God surely could heal any one of them. And yet, he does not always restore. And that brings us full circle to the "why not." Because God does his greatest, most permanent work in our lives when we are tested by the fires. He won't let your fire consume you, but he will let it refine you.

Comfort through Our Trials

And now the promised scripture that can provide great comfort in the midst of our trials. But you'll see it's done a bit differently than previous scripture texts. I want you to read through them as one cohesive unit, uninterrupted by the scripture reference. You'll find them footnoted below.

> "Blessed is the man who remains steadfast under trial, for when he has stood the test he will receive the crown of life, which God has promised to those who love him.[2] And after you have suffered a little while, the God of all grace, who has called you to his eternal glory in Christ, will himself restore, confirm, strengthen, and establish you.[3]

> "I have said these things to you, that in me you may have peace. In the world you will have tribulation. But take heart; I have overcome the world. [4] Count it all joy, my brothers, when you meet trials of various kinds, for you know that the testing of your faith produces steadfastness.[5]

> "Not only that, but we rejoice in our sufferings, knowing that suffering produces endurance, and endurance produces character, and character produces hope… [6] Beloved, do not be surprised at the fiery trial when it comes upon you to test you, as though something strange were happening to you. But rejoice insofar as you share Christ's sufferings, that you may also rejoice and be glad when his glory is revealed. [7]

> "For I consider that the sufferings of this present time are not worth comparing with the glory that is to be revealed to us. [8] In this you rejoice, though now for a little while, if necessary, you have been grieved by various trials, so that the tested genuineness of your faith—more precious than gold that perishes though it is tested by fire—may be found to result in praise and glory and honor at the revelation of Jesus Christ.[9]

> "So we do not lose heart. Though our outer self is wasting away, our inner self is being renewed day by day. For this light momentary affliction is preparing for us an eternal weight of glory beyond all comparison."[10]

I hope you were able to let the truth of those verses wash over you like a balm for your soul. Our great God *is* a God of comfort and his Word reminds us of that again and again. These verses remind me of one more way our trials bring good into our lives – without them, we would never experience God's incredible comfort through them.

And so "the honest griever" begins to see how God does his best and most permanent work.

16

Scripture Revelations

I've been looking forward to these last two chapters in this section for weeks. Long before I knew what the book structure or content would be, I *knew* these two chapters would be well represented. How could I not include the very events that helped me get up every morning for years? Or helped me get out of my puddle of tears? Or so filled me with wonder that I knew I must share them with anyone who would listen?

Seeing God's hand on my life, whether it be opening my eyes to new scripture meaning, or by showing up in unexpected ways, was the key to survival. Having ears to hear and eyes to see his work was crucial to any healing he wanted to impart. There would be no looking for blessings through trials if God hadn't given me regular doses of his presence in my life – and the ability to recognize them.

These next two chapters will be filled with the blog posts that chronicle those revelations. In most cases, I was headed down a very wrong road theologically (what one believes about God), and granting me these new eyes to see put me back on the healing path. Maybe these revelations won't be new to you, and if so, then I'm delighted you've already arrived at these truths. But if not, I pray that my scripture revelations can also be yours, and that they will bring awe and wonder to your life as they did to mine.

Scriptural "Aha" Moments

For a change, I'm going to share these posts in chronological order to see how this new level of understanding grew over time, and built upon the previously gained knowledge. I believe they will all speak for themselves with no introductions needed.

"The Power of the Cross"

Day 165

A week or so ago, I was sending a YouTube video of the song, "The Power of the Cross" to some prospective choir members in our church, in hopes that they would join us on Easter morning in singing this amazing song.

A similar group sang this for an Easter service at our church out in Earlham ten years ago. And because we all loved it so much, it became a favorite of the congregation and we added it to our repertoire. We even did the full-blown choir version! So, I'm extremely familiar with this song as I've sung and/or played it dozens of times.

So, I was completely caught off guard when, while I was half-viewing the YouTube before sending it, I just broke down into tears as I was moved by the words of the verse I was hearing. But do you think I can remember which verse it was now? Of course not ... I reread them all just now and decided that any one of them could create the same reaction because they are all extremely powerful – and *true*!

The thought that slammed into my mind and caused the flood of tears was this: Jesus went through the agony of the cross, both physically and spiritually (in that he experienced separation from his heavenly Father), *so that* I would have the joy of seeing my husband again one day. It makes me cry again even now.

And while that is an incredible promise and what I often cling to during this time of grieving, it really is *not* what we can best celebrate in heaven. Yes, it's a huge comfort to think about seeing our loved ones again, because, let's face it, what or who could be more tangible to us than the people we have loved the most and lost? And let's not forget the biblical promise of no more tears and no more sorrow and no more pain. Boy, do I long for *that*!

But if you're a believer, our greatest joy lies in the indisputable fact that our Savior, Jesus Christ, the same one who went to the cross on our behalf, is reigning triumphantly in heaven, seated at the right hand of God the Father and we can now be in his presence *forever*! There can be no greater joy than to spend eternity in paradise with the one who sacrificed it all for us. And the icing on that heavenly cake? We also reunite with our believing loved ones – and no more sorrow, pain, or tears.

Although this song focuses on Christ's death on the cross, the greatest news in the history of the world is that he rose again! No other world religion has a leader who died and came back to life *on our behalf*! It's an amazing truth of the Gospel and one that I hope and pray you will be able to embrace this Easter weekend.

Christ didn't stay on the cross, but the penalty for our sins did if we acknowledge him as Lord and Savior of our lives. If we don't, then there is no power in that cross for us. Our part in this salvation story is to recognize that we "all have sinned and fall short of the glory of God" (Romans 3:23). And then what? "If we confess our sins, he is faithful and just to forgive us our sins and to cleanse us from all unrighteousness" (1 John 1:9).

There you have it. Direct from the mouth of God! Don't put off this decision if you haven't made it yet. None of us knows if we will see tomorrow. But we can face it with hope, as Dale did, if we've claimed Christ's sacrifice as our own.

Have a blessed Easter because *Christ is risen*!

"Vacation Re-entry ... and a New Hope"

Day 207

For those of you who saw my recent Facebook pix, you know that I took a vacation to Phoenix, Arizona with some girlfriends. These are friends from *way* back in my early days with Northwestern Bell – which became USWest, which became Qwest, which became Century Link. We've been friends since 1983 and I'm *so* blessed that they are still such a big part of my life. It's the kind of friendship that can pick up where we left off and not miss a beat.

We did all the fun things you do on vacation – lots of pool time, a little *hot* golf, dinners out, trip to Sedona, sleeping in, and *lots* of chocolate and laughter. Such an encouraging time for me. How ironic that I would find a respite from the emotional desert in which I find myself – in that desert! But it was a wonderful solace for my soul.

Most of us know there is a somewhat depressing re-entry time after a vacation – or even after a nice, long weekend. It means we go back to the reality of work or school or chores or problems or whatever. It's not my favorite part of a vacation and I'm sure it's not yours.

But this re-entry was *hard*! The reality I faced after this trip was "full of emptiness" (intentional pun) and sadness. I so wanted to call Dale and tell him about my trip. Despite the dogs' exuberance at my return, the house seemed noticeably quiet and lonely. I found myself tearful for three to four days after my return.

My grief centered around the loss of this great love we had. Like any relationship that is decades long, our love went through numerous stages. There's the beginning stage of new love with a little bit of infatuation thrown in. The kind where you just can't stop thinking about him and feel incomplete whenever you're apart. It must be one of the most exciting times in a relationship and ours was no different. As the years went by, of course we worked through the issues that are bound to crop up in a relationship and marriage.

And yet, so much of that initial love remained for me throughout our marriage. The bonus was that we added to that the deep, abiding love that grows *because* of what you've been through together. I learned that I could *always* count on Dale's love and I would trust him with anything.

I know how blessed I am to be able to claim that in my marriage. But, of course, the flip side is that the pain of that loss is so deep. As believers, the great hope we have is to see our loved ones again and spend eternity together before the throne of God.

That has been my hope as I lost grandparents, parents, aunts and uncles, and friends throughout my life. Those relationships would all be restored one day, and I found great comfort in that promise.

But I wasn't feeling the same level of comfort when I thought about reuniting with Dale one day. I know that sounds crazy, so let me explain how I landed there. The Bible says in Matthew 20:30, "For in the resurrection they neither marry nor are given in marriage, but are like the angels in heaven."

I've known the truth behind this passage for most of my adult life. Dale and I would *not* be husband and wife in heaven. I won't take the time in this post to get into all the nitty-gritty of that, but briefly - marriage is not necessary in heaven. All believers constitute the

Church of Christ and we are all Christ's bride. It's a great picture of what marriage is really all about and it comes to a perfect conclusion in eternity.

So, what was my problem? My love for Dale was the deepest love I have ever experienced in my life and when he died, it felt like my heart was ripped out. I knew I would never again experience 35 years of that unconditional love, the kind that you can only have with a spouse.

And because of the "no-marriage-in-heaven" clause, it seemed as though my relationship with Dale, once I reached heaven, would be lessened somehow. I imagined it would be more like getting to see a long-lost friend again, or even a parent. And that's not what I wanted! I wanted to enjoy that deep love between a husband and wife for eternity.

Hence the extra sadness and, to a certain degree, hopelessness that I felt based on my assumption that I would never have this love again ... ever.

It's remarkable how one can sit under solid biblical teaching for so many years and still get some of the theology wrong! And I'll admit it's a little embarrassing to have overlooked what should have been so clear to me. Thankfully, God decided to straighten me out – and I'm so glad he did! I don't hear an actual voice of God, but I often get such a strong sense of what he wants me to know that there's no doubt in my mind, or soul, that it is from him.

That was the case as I was having that little pity party about never being able to experience this unique love with Dale again. God *clearly* "spoke" to me and said, "The love you will have with Dale in heaven will be *so* much more than anything you ever experienced here on earth with him, and more than you could possibly imagine with your limited knowledge in this life."

Boom! (I've always wanted to use that!) My lightning bolt hit. Of course, God would *never* have our experiences in heaven be anything less than perfection! It is his pure agape love that will be present in every relationship we will have, especially our relationship with *him*! Agape love is what we see in 1 Corinthians 13, often known as the love chapter. It is *everything* we would ever want love to be, and that's what God has in store for us.

Any of us who attended church or Sunday School as children learned this simple truth – God is love. He is so much more than that, but love defines him and as 1 Corinthians 13 says, "So now faith, love and hope abide, these three; but the greatest of these is love." So, of course God, the perfect embodiment of love, will get it perfectly right!

Okay, I get it now! Yes, I will still be so sad in this life that I won't share that love with Dale on this side of Glory. But, oh what hope I have that the heavenly, agape love waiting for us will absolutely blow my socks off!

These are the kinds of revelations God gives to me on this journey that remind me how much he does love me, and continues to walk with me and teach me what I'd likely never learn without this season. Talk about trading sorrow for joy, tears for laughter, and hopelessness for a hopeful expectation.

I think I'll officially declare this particular pity party over... Thanks be to God!

"What About Joy?"

Day 244

Recently, I've had several friends ask me to pray that God would bring joy into their lives daily, particularly through their trials. Or through the trials of their loved ones. Let's face it, in today's world, we are bombarded, surrounded, inundated, and overwhelmed with gloom and doom. One must almost unplug from the world to get some relief, it seems.

I can absolutely relate to that. There is so much in this world that can steal our joy. For me, it's all the above, and the trials of grieving through Dale's death. Some days it feels as though joy has taken a holiday somewhere besides my house, or this world.

So, I thought this would be an appropriate topic for today's post. Consequently, as I often do, I started some research to see what certain writers and pastors had to say about this topic. I'm not looking for any pat answers; I want to see what theologians I trust say. And then apply that to my life and hopefully to yours.

Much of what I read was not new and just confirmed what I've believed about joy for years now. And one concept I believed is that happiness is a much more "secular" goal – who doesn't want to be happy? Many of the graduation snippets I've heard lately feature speakers who are trying to guide the new graduates in their quest for happiness. Contrast that temporary feeling with the deep, abiding concept of joy – a feeling that we can abide in, no matter what our circumstances. Spiritually, I'd say that this type of joy, in its purest sense, can best be supplied by God.

You can imagine my surprise when I came upon a radio interview with Randy Alcorn (Alcorn, Daniel Di Bartolo, *Faithlife Today*, Feb. 3, 2016) a few years ago where he turns this whole concept of happiness being secular and joy being spiritual on its head!

My church teaches that when we have a framework/scripture collision, scripture must win out. In other words, if what I've believed about something does not match up with what I now clearly see in scripture, guess what needs to change? Certainly not God's Word! I must adjust my thinking.

That's exactly what I've just done in the past hour or so. The premise of this radio interview was that the words "joy" and "happiness" in all the various Hebrew and Greek transcripts are essentially *interchangeable*. They are synonyms for each other again and again and again in both the Old and New Testaments, along with words like "gladness" and "contentment."

So, whether you buy into that thought at this point or not, stay with me as I look into some other nuggets of truth from God's Word on this topic of joy:

God's Word commands us to be joyful. Many times! Yikes! That feels impossible, right? If we're just trying to muster up this joyful feeling, no wonder that's not working for us, at least not long-term. We can't do it! So, if we stop there, it's no wonder we are frustrated and feel like attaining joy is an impossible task.

What supplies our joy? Is it the circumstances surrounding us? Our job, our mental and physical health, our relationships, our finances, other blessings in our lives? Yep, I must confess – for me, those areas often dictate how joyful, or happy I feel.

Let me suggest that we can still find joy and happiness in all those areas I listed above. And I believe it is right to do so. When things are going well, rejoice! But wouldn't we love to land where Paul did, as he states in his letter to the Philippians? "I have learned in whatever situation I am to be content" (Philippians 4:11).

How do we get there? Psalm 37:4 gives us one answer: "Delight yourself in the Lord, and he will give you the desires of your heart." As believers, it's as simple and as complicated as that. If we start to switch our focus to the character of God and all that he has done for us through the sacrifice of his Son, Jesus on the cross, our "momentary troubles" can start to shrink in comparison.

Specifically, can we rest and find joy knowing that God is sovereign over all things? Does this give us peace? If so, camp out there for a while!

Do we find God's Spirit speaking as we read his Word or go to him in prayer? Is fellowship with him sweet? If so, savor that – rinse and repeat!

Do we value Christ above all else? Honestly, that's a tough one, isn't it? We want to say we do, and hope that we can eventually achieve that, but much of the things of this world can leapfrog over Christ and his supremacy.

Let me share a recent lesson I learned. If you've read earlier posts, you know that I had to put my sweet dog, Missy, to sleep a few weeks ago. About a week ago, my other dog, Daisy, got violently ill with vomiting, resulting in another trip to the emergency vet over the weekend. She ended up staying there from Sunday until this past Wednesday morning as they treated her for pancreatitis and gastroenteritis, along with severe dehydration. She was seriously one sick puppy.

I came home to so much quiet – no Dale, no Missy, and no Daisy. Through my tears, I pleaded with God not to take my Daisy. Surely, he would not do that after I've lost so much this year. Gratefully, he did *not* take Daisy and I'm happy (and joyful) to report that she is home and very much on the mend.

But it caused me to think about what my response would have been if God had, in fact, chosen to take Daisy as well. I seriously told people that I would just be done ... But would I? What would the proper response be to another loss like that? What would God be teaching me? We really can't know the mind of God; however, I did have to honestly ask myself, could it be that I cherish things of this world (my husband, my pets) *more* than God himself? Might that be his lesson? Yikes again …

It was a good reminder to me and maybe for you that our greatest joy and happiness lie in our relationship with Jesus Christ, and in trusting in the supremacy of God's sovereignty.

This sounds sweet, right? So, getting back to an earlier question: why do we still find it so difficult? I ask myself often, "Am I trying to do this in my own strength?" And almost as often, the answer is, "Yes!" If God commands us to be joyful and to delight ourselves in him, then, through his Holy Spirit, he can surely supply it for us, if we allow him to work that out in our lives.

Even knowing this, doesn't necessarily mean we master it perfectly. But we need to put aside our strong desire to fix everything ourselves, in our own lives and in the lives of our loved ones. And meditate on the scriptural fact that God's Holy Spirit in us can accomplish all things, even giving us *joy* in the midst of trials. Or in the midst of our own self-improvement project. Let him be God and let him sanctify you with the joy he so wants you to experience.

Book after book have been written on the subject of joy, and innumerable sermons preached on the topic, so this humble little blog post can't possibly even scratch the surface of all that God's Word says about joy and happiness.

So, go to God's Word and search for scriptures related to this subject and then just let those truths wash over you and give you hope. If you don't have a personal relationship with Jesus Christ and have never been able to find lasting joy in anything you've pursued, maybe now is the time to hear God's voice calling you.

Let me leave you with one scripture text that beautifully summarizes much of what I hope and pray this post has challenged you with.

"May the God of hope fill you with all
joy and peace as you trust in him,
so that you may overflow with
hope by the power of the Holy Spirit."
Romans 15:13

"I Don't Have *That* Sorrow"

Day 437

As I write this, Christmas is just starting to appear in the rearview mirror – New Year's is straight ahead. How did your holiday season go? Boy, we all have stories from that, don't we?

Mine was definitely a mixed bag. Some very tearful times as this was my first Christmas at home without Dale. And yet some times of blessing, too, with friends and family.

But this post is not about the holidays. I'm moving on from those quickly. Grateful to have survived! I want to share a revelation, of sorts, that I had while reading one of my daily devotions in *Streams in the Desert* (Zondervan, rev. 1999) this past week.

This one was encouraging the reader to know that God is always by our side no matter what we might be feeling. The author asked the questions, "Do you feel like God has turned his back on you? Do you feel unloved by God? Does it seem like he doesn't care about what you're going through? Do you feel forsaken by him?"

I could honestly, and gratefully, answer, "No, I do *not* feel like that!" Despite the great sorrow and loss of this past year – and other difficult times in my life – I do not doubt God's love for me. I rest fully in the promises I find in his Word. They are what sustain me in my darkest moments. And for that, I am eternally grateful to God.

Because, ultimately, he is the one who has blessed me with that faith. It's nothing that I've conjured up out of my own strength. It is something that he has mercifully bestowed upon me. Oh sure, it definitely helps that I have sat under solid biblical teaching for years. And that helped me get my theology (what I believe about God) in place before the deepest trials hit.

But I can take no credit for it. If you find yourself answering, "Yes" to any of those questions posed earlier, I do have some encouragement for you.

I must take you to another Christian holiday to illustrate my point. Fast forward to Easter, or more accurately, Good Friday. If you've ever read the excruciating details of what Jesus physically suffered through the scourging and eventual death by crucifixion, you know that it's about as bad as anything can get.

But an even deeper suffering that Christ endured was evidenced by His words on the cross that fateful day; "My God, my God, why have you forsaken me?" When Jesus took the weight and the penalty of our sins on that cross, God *did* forsake him while that penalty was being paid.

But back to the devotional. As I read the comforting words about God never forsaking us – and my gratitude that I trusted in his presence – I realized that it was *because* Jesus was forsaken on that cross, that I don't need to ever feel alone in this life. I may be suffering from many other sources of sorrow, but I don't have *that* sorrow.

He paved that way for us to have unbroken fellowship with God forever, if we confess our sins and ask him to be Lord of our lives. He has already done the heavy lifting.

So, when you start to question whether God loves you or would ever forsake you, be reminded of the great lengths and depths Jesus went to so that you could be spared that kind of sorrow. Please don't take it lightly. He wants us to fully trust his promise that he will never leave us or forsake us. It's not just a simple platitude; it's a truth born out of Jesus' suffering on our behalf.

Now there's a Christmas/Good Friday gift that we can all be grateful for! May you know that truth as you finish out 2018 and head into a new year.

"Be strong and courageous. Do not fear or be in dread of them,
for it is the Lord your God who goes with you.
He will not leave you or forsake you."
Deuteronomy 31:6

"Feelings ... Nothing More Than Feelings"

Day 541

One of the downsides of being a musician is that almost everything reminds me of a song. You must go all the way back to 1975 for this one. For those of you who know it, I apologize already if it became an ear worm for you! If you don't know it, count your blessings ...

But "feelings" is one of the topics I want to discuss in today's blog post. This may resonate a bit more with the female gender, but I do hope there's something here for everyone.

I don't know about you all, but for as long as I can remember, I would take an inventory of my day every night when I went to bed. That's when I would scroll through the activities and emotions of the day that had come to an end and settle on a rating of mostly good or mostly bad.

And that rating would often dictate if I felt happy or sad about the day. From there, I would generally head into my prayer time and talk with God about my day. This conversation ranged from gratefulness for a good day, to repentance over any of my thoughts or actions that were less than kind, to pleading with God for something I felt I needed, to intercession for someone else's needs. And often it was a complicated mixture of all of that.

I'm grateful that the happy endings of those days far outweighed the sad ones. But the point is, my emotions dictated whether I felt good or bad about the past 24 hours. And I honestly never thought there was any other way to gauge the success or failure of my day.

Enter ... widowhood.

I still do a sort of emotional inventory at the end of my days. And I have some of those same conversations with God. But regardless of the kind of day I've had, or the good times or joy I've experienced, once I'm left alone with my emotions as I retire for the day, there is *always* sadness.

It's not what I want, but it's what's left when the busyness of the day is stripped away. I can't not (yes, I want the double negative here ...) miss Dale in the depths of my soul at the end of each day for the past nearly18 months. It's when the tears come and when the heartache is deep and profound. For me, it's when the real work of grieving is done.

Enter ... hope

It's also where I've learned to lean the most on God. And not only am I leaning on him, but I've begun to *focus* on his character and his promises. It's where I put the emotions aside and rest in the knowledge that I am a Child of God. That he loves me with an everlasting love. That he wants only good for my life, even if that comes through pain. It's where I'm reminded that he will make *everything* right in the end.

And maybe most importantly, I understand that the emotions I'm feeling don't change his character or his promises one iota. I am not defined by my emotions. I am defined by who I am in Christ. And I find joy and hope in the promises he so clearly lays out for me in his Word.

Emotions really are fleeting. One or two silly events can send us soaring to the mountaintop, or crashing down into the valley. It can be an exhausting way to live. And it isn't what God wants for us.

I'm not saying we ignore our emotions, or fail to validate someone else's. God did create us with those emotions. What I am proposing, however, is that we limit the power they have over us by switching our focus to *God's* power. When you feel your emotions sending you on a downward spiral, consciously and purposefully meditate on the Good News of the Gospel.

I can tell you it's the *only* way that I bring some balance into my emotional life. And when your days end with sadness, you too can be filled with hope again if you focus on the only one who can bring true happiness.

"Do not be conformed to this world, but be transformed by the renewal of your mind,that by testing you may discern what is the will of God,what is good and acceptable and perfect."
Romans 12:2

"Living in the Moment?"

Day 717

I bet you expect this to be a post about how we should enjoy all the many moments that make up this crazy life of ours. Easy to live in the past or the future and not appreciate what we have in the "now."

That is absolutely a wonderful concept and one that I have written about in the past. This post, however, is *not* about that kind of "living in the moment." My version in this post will have a completely different twist!

To set up just how this new revelation made its way into my life recently, I must share some of what I've been experiencing for the past month or two.

I'm working diligently on the launch of my book, *Cultivating Compassion – Practical Advice as You Walk a Friend through a Season of Loss*. Let me just say the writing of the book was the *easiest* part of this process!

Enter the world of self-publishing on Amazon. Honestly, it's a sub-culture unto itself. But I am taking a course to help me learn all the ins and outs of Amazon's algorithms and how to utilize them most effectively.

Unfortunately, that means *lots* of new technology for someone who often describes herself as walking around with a black technology cloud over her head. Yep, that's me. Not too beneficial for this stage of things.

So, I have been banging my head against the wall, taking one step forward and two steps back, and any other adage you can use to describe a high level of frustration and an incredibly low level of productivity. On more than one occasion, it has led to tears and the temptation to throw in the towel. (Hey, another adage!)

All that led me to the realization that I was living *too much* in those moments. I was letting the frustration of the daily struggles color my entire outlook on life. It caused me to take a huge step backwards, but in a good, self-reflecting sense.

So, I had to ask myself, "What difference will this particular problem make in the scope of eternity?" Might it delay the launch of the book? Maybe. Might it cause a few restless nights? For sure! But I had to remind myself, once again, that this ministry belongs to God. And his purposes for it will go forward regardless of any technical glitches I may run into.

And here's the other thing – God, the *all-knowing* God, has the answers to every one of those technology problems. He's got this. And he'll lead me to answers and resolutions in his timing.

So, I needed to *stop* living in those moments of frustration and towel-throwing, and remember just who it is I'm serving. Keep my eye on the big picture, knowing that I'm not in charge. *And*, keep my eye on the eternal picture. All these frustrations pale in comparison to what's ahead at the end of this earthly life.

I pray you can also learn to cherish the beautiful moments, but hand over your difficult times to a good God.

"Finally, brothers, whatever is true, whatever is honorable, whatever is just, whatever is pure,whatever is lovely, whatever is commendable, if there is any excellence,if there is anything worthy of praise, think about these things."
Philippians 4:8

That's quite a collection, isn't it? I enjoyed reading through them all again because the totality of them all back-to-back highlighted the incredible magnitude of all those revelations. And as time has passed, this greater understanding has become part of who I am as a Christian because God stretches me every time he gives me new insights. It's one gigantic praise during this season of widowhood. One I wouldn't have without this journey.

I hope that you're able to take these revelations and apply them to your own life situation. Even if they aren't all new to you, perhaps the application is. This truly is the practical application of God's Word in our lives. Find areas where these truths can speak hope into your hurting world. Then experience how God can change you into a deeper, wiser sufferer.

And so "the honest griever" begins to live out the promises made in God's Word.

17

When God Moves

To be clear, God is *always* on the move! None of us can fathom all that he is doing every second of every day in the countless human lives down through the ages. Mind boggling doesn't come close to describing that reality.

So, this title and chapter are specifically looking at the times in the past few years when the events were so awe-inspiring that they could only be from God's hand. And more specifically – God opening my eyes to see what he was doing.

I've been a believer since I was 14 years old and I've never so clearly seen God's hand on my life as I have in these past few years. It amazes me; it comforts me; it reminds me of God's presence and love for me; and ultimately it causes me to love him even more. But the reality is that it took an event like my husband's death for me to see God moving in such specific ways. Is it because I wasn't paying attention before? Maybe ... Or maybe, this is another way that God chooses to bless me in my days of mourning.

I'm honored to share these stories with you and pray that they encourage you, or even cause you to take a second look at this great God, if you've doubted his existence or interest in our everyday lives. Once again, a chronological order is the most effective way for each story to build upon the previous one.

His Final Earthly Home

To see the full impact of this story, I must go back to the fall of 2013. We had just suffered through that horrible year with all of Dale's health problems and a slew of other challenges. I was scheduled to go on a girlfriend trip to Florida in February 2014, but knowing how sick Dale was, I told them I just couldn't join them. But the shoe we thought was going to drop after a trip to Mayo Clinic never fell, and I started to cautiously hope I might still be able to make the trip.

Dale improved significantly, but not to the extent that I felt he could be home alone for a week. So, I started calling around to find a care facility that would do respite care. Not as easy as you might think! But I did find a facility that felt respite care was incredibly important for family members. So Dale and I got in the car and headed out. We met the management staff and had a complete tour of the facility including the room he was likely to occupy.

As we were leaving, I asked him what he thought of it. He decided it would be a great place to stay for a week and didn't think I should do any more checking around. Done deal! I had a much-needed respite of my own in Florida and Dale got along splendidly during his own respite.

Fast-forward to the fall of 2016. Dale's dementia has now declined to the point where I clearly can't keep him safe at home. So I start what would become a grueling process of finding an appropriate home for him during his final days.

Of course, the first call I made was to his respite home from 2014. Sorry, no openings. Not expecting any.

The next few months were spent "secretly" calling or visiting virtually every care facility in the metro area. I won't bore you with all the reasons that essentially everything fell through. Even when I thought the perfect option had opened for us, it, too, fell apart at the last minute. I was in tears, again secretly, for weeks during this process.

After that last disappointment, I took a few days off for my pity party, and then planned to start contacting care facilities in the surrounding small communities. But before I did, I thought I'd make one more call to the original facility from his respite visit. Imagine my surprise when the director said, "Why don't you come and see us? We have some things changing in the next few weeks." What??

So, I rushed over there to find out that, yes, they expected a room to open within the next 30 days. I could barely contain my relief and joy and gratitude! The care facility where Dale would spend his last ten months on this earth was the *exact* place he had picked out for himself almost three years earlier.

He already knew the layout; he knew the staff; he liked the food; he was happy with the room set-up. In short, it was the *perfect* solution, and so much better than anything I had been trying to "land" all those many weeks.

When things fall into place like this, it confirms not only the correctness of this decision, but it also reminds me that God loves us both and had this picture in mind all along. He cared about these details in our life and I couldn't have been more grateful.

Godly Confirmation

I have purposely not shared yet what the faith part of our marriage looked like because it belongs in *this* story. As I mentioned, I have been a believer in Jesus Christ since I was 14 years old, and my faith in God is at the core of who I am. When Dale and I started dating, I knew he believed in God and we attended church together. That's all I needed at that point.

Not long after we got married, I started attending a powerful Bible study that challenged me personally in my faith and caused me to look at Dale's faith more closely as well. Despite his belief in God, I wasn't sure that he had a *saving* faith through Jesus.

It became one of the few challenges in our marriage through the years. We didn't pray together, we didn't have any deep discussions about God, and we didn't see eye-to-eye on what this saving faith should look like. I must admit that I vacillated between wanting to be a silent witness through my actions ("*they [husbands] may be won without a word by the conduct of their wives*" [1 Peter 3:9b]) and wanting to nag him into believing ("*Better to live in a desert than with a quarrelsome and nagging wife*" [Proverbs 21:19]).

I often felt that Dale had the head-knowledge, but not the necessary heart-knowledge. As he got older, the idea of never seeing him again after he died brought me to tears repeatedly. I would often plead with God, "I know you don't owe me this, but somehow let me know that he is going to heaven."

During those last ten months before he died, I did bring the subject up again and he assured me that he knew he was going to heaven. I said to him, "Well, I guess I just have to trust that." That was the last time we talked about it.

Within a few weeks he was gone, and there was nothing more to be said on that subject. Or so I thought. That first night after he died, I alternated between desperately trying to sleep, and then going to my Bible app to read through scripture.

Somewhere around 4:00 a.m., God led me to this scripture, "Precious in the sight of the Lord is the death of his saints" (Psalm 116:15). The biblical definition of "saint" is anyone who is a true believer. *This* was the moment that God graciously let me know that he had, indeed, taken Dale home to be with him in heaven.

I can't begin to tell you how powerful that revelation was in the middle of that sleepless night. What joy it brought during my darkest hours, when that confirmation would have the greatest impact in my life. It informs my view of life after death and is *key* to the comfort I receive from anticipating our glorious reunion one day.

My Fur Babies' Heartbreak and Joy

I am a *huge* animal lover and have been since before I could walk. I have had pets – mostly Boston Terriers or Boston mixes my entire life. I don't have children of my own, but my pets fully take on that role in my world. Because I knew marrying Dale meant I wouldn't have children, I would often tell him, "If I ever go through a stage where I want to have a baby, just get me another dog." Seriously.

So these next two posts will likely pull on your heart strings a bit, especially if you love animals like I do. Even if you don't, I believe you will still see God's hand on this season of my life. Here it is in two parts.

"Good-Bye Sweet Missy"

Day 223

Reader beware. This will *not* be a happy post. So, you may want to save this for another time if you're in the middle of having fun this holiday weekend.

I had to make the heart wrenching decision to put my sweet Missy to sleep today. And since I have been working through my grief and pain of losing Dale through this blog, I figured why not continue the therapy here? Anyone that knows me for more than a day will understand that my pets have always been like children to me. Yes, I am that crazy, over-the-top animal lover that many of you may not quite understand. And you won't understand the depth of my grief. But you fellow animal lovers will completely get this.

Missy came to us about five years ago after the painful, tragic loss of our Boston Terrier, Holly. We really didn't intend on getting another dog so quickly, but six days after losing Holly, we had our little Missy girl to help us grieve. We were never sure what her first six years looked like, but clearly she came from an abusive background. Despite five years of nothing but love and kindness with us, she was still afraid of the leash, still tensed up anytime I picked her up, and still bore some scars on her precious little body.

But regardless of that past, she had the sweetest personality of *any* dog I have ever had. And that's saying something, because I've had some great dogs throughout my life. She didn't seem to be afraid of people or other animals, always greeting whomever came to the door. She would wait patiently in the background while Daisy hogged all the attention. Then it's like she'd say, "Hey, maybe you could just give me a little pet, if it's not too much trouble!"

It's always amazing to me how animals can continue to trust us humans even when we've caused them pain. We can learn a *lot* from that. I'm so grateful that we had her for as long as we did. I always told people that Missy would be the perfect dog for anyone who didn't like dogs, because she was just that precious.

She entered a household that was run by Crazy Daisy and they were a perfect match. Missy needed a leader and Daisy needed another minion for her kingdom. They were complete opposites and yet, perfectly paired. God's hand was clearly guiding the process of getting Missy into this home. I'm grateful that Dale and I, along with our family and friends, could be the ones to show her what her life was supposed to be.

About a month ago, she started having some heart issues and was put on medication. I was also to keep an eye on her breathing rate and get her back to the vet if it was over 40 breaths per minute. She had been running around 20, so no worries here.

Last Thursday, her breathing took a turn for the worse and she clocked in at 60 breaths per minute. At her vet appointment the next day, her X-rays showed a lot of fluid in and around her lungs. A shot of Lasix and some water pills were our last hope to give her some relief, as she was clearly in distress with such rapid breathing. I left for the holiday weekend with instructions to take her to the emergency vet if her breathing didn't return to 40/minute by 9:00 p.m. that night. It did not, but I wasn't ready to let her go.

I wanted to give the medication a day or so to see if it would help before making that final decision. By last night, it was clearly not working for her and I knew what lie ahead for us.

In the 31 years that Dale and I were married, he was the one who always did the hard work of taking our pets to the vet when their time had come. I would stay home, lost in my tears and grief. Dale would always, sometimes a *bit* grudgingly, agree to get another dog, so that's one of the ways that we would begin our healing process.

Now that Dale is gone, the decision fell to me – and even more importantly, the *job* fell to me. I did have dear friends who offered to go with me and to them I say, "Thank you for being willing to grieve this with me!" But I knew what a basket case I would become, and I just needed to do that in the privacy of my own little world.

So, I made Daisy give Missy a last wet kiss, and off we went to the emergency vet clinic. I won't take you through all those tearful details, but will tell you that it's a very peaceful process, if you've never been through it. Peaceful, but final.

The pain of losing a beloved pet, especially for us crazy animal lovers, is one of the worst things you go through. So, to have to deal with this while I'm still deep in the grieving process of losing Dale just doubled the pain. Of course, I missed him not being here to do that hard work, but I also missed not having him here to grieve with.

But, as sad as this time is, and as much of a downer as this blog post is, I did have an extremely sweet thought that brings me some comfort. I picture Missy waking up in heaven and running into Dale's open arms! What a precious homecoming that would be! Can't you just see it?

I know, I know – the Bible does *not* tell us that our pets will be there. But it *does* say that all creation will one day be restored. And we know the Garden of Eden was full of animals, so I fully expect to see animals there. I love what Randy Alcorn says in his book *Heaven* (Tyndale Momentum, 2011), "Wouldn't it be just like God to have our pets in heaven?" Yes, yes, it would! So *that's* what I'm going with. I may be wrong, but I'm going to hang onto that picture and that hope as I continue to grieve both losses.

If I haven't made you cry yet, here's my last chance. My last words to Missy before she was gone were, "I love you, my sweet girl. Now go run to Daddy." That's what I want to remember.

"A Gift Named Winnie"

Day 250

Happy post! Some of you have probably seen a recent Facebook post showing off my new little dog, Winnie. This is such a cool story that I wanted to put a little meat on the bones of that picture, so you can see how God blesses his children in the midst of their trials.

Just to refresh, I made the difficult, but correct decision to put my sweet Missy down a few weeks ago. And two weeks to the day after that, I was back at the same emergency vet with an extremely sick Daisy, who wasn't to return home for another three days.

So, adding those two tearful events into a life that was already quite tearful seemed overwhelming to me at the time. But all ended well for Daisy and she is back to her normal crazy self. (I was kind of hoping to take a little of the crazy off, but no such luck ...)

Long before Dale passed away, we had discussed downsizing the number of pets we had, which was two dogs and a cat. Eventually I would want to be in a townhome that would not have a fenced back yard. So, we both agreed that once Missy was gone, we would become a one-dog-one-cat household.

And I was absolutely okay with that. I know that's hard for some of you to believe ... but it's true! I think this must go along with aging, but I found myself wondering how many more dogs I would have in this life, and how many more cars. That's right, dogs and cars. Anybody else find themselves doing that?? So, I had the math all figured out and agreed that this would be the time to start the downsizing process in the dog world.

I came home from dinner last Friday night and checked my Facebook newsfeed before going to bed. What would show up but an adorable Boston/Frenchie face named Winnie who was needing a home? The post was from a friend named Lynn whom I met through the Boston Terrier rescue almost eight years ago. She lives in Iowa City and we had never met in person. Winnie was five years old, surrendered from a home, got along great with kids, other dogs and cats, and was so, so sweet.

Huh ... what do I do with *that*? Well, I did send a private message to Lynn asking, "Do I need to talk to you about this dog??"

Then I prayed that God would either open doors for me to adopt her, or clearly shut them by giving her to someone else.

The next morning, I called Lynn and we chatted a bit about Winnie's personality and her history. It all seemed *so* right, especially the part about Winnie *not* being a strong alpha dog. Can't have two of those in this household. But one problem. I couldn't get Daisy over to Iowa City to meet Winnie because she has become terrified of riding in the car the past few years. (In fact, that is exactly what I was working on when I erroneously gave her too many hot dog treats resulting in her trip to the emergency vet. Word to the wise ...)

I asked Lynn if she thought it would be enough for me to come meet Winnie in Iowa City and then decide if her personality seemed compatible with Daisy's. To which she replied, "We will be in Des Moines tomorrow and can bring Winnie along. I can help introduce them." WOW! Can you say, "Door. Wide. Open?"

So, at 11:30 a.m. the next day, Lynn showed up with Winnie and it was love at first sight for me. Such a happy, loving little girl! But now the big test. Introduce her to Daisy. So off to the back yard we went awaiting the big meet-and-greet. When I brought Daisy out, there were a few seconds of some fairly aggressive sniffing and then ... that's it! No signs of stress or aggression in either dog. That, in itself, is a minor miracle, as those of you who know Daisy might attest!

By noon, it was a done deal (minus the follow-up paperwork) and Winnie had found a new home. She slipped immediately into a comfortable routine here, getting along great with both Daisy *and* the cat, Max. He quickly decided that she was no threat and has already started trying to play with her a bit.

As I was looking through all of Winnie's paperwork, I found the original document from when the previous owners had purchased her and, surprise (?), she came from the same breeder as Daisy! One more confirmation that this was absolutely the right decision. Winnie was meant to be part of this family.

I couldn't help but be amazed at how all of this transpired so quickly, and so clearly! While I truly had no intentions of getting another dog, God obviously had different plans. I started to see the blessing that this was in my life, after some very difficult weeks and months. Winnie was God's gift to me, when I wasn't expecting it.

How good and kind is our God? It brings tears to my eyes (happy ones) when I think of the depth of his love for me to bring this little punkin into my life when I didn't even know that I needed her. But God did, and chose to bless me beyond what I could have hoped for.

> *"If you then, being evil, know how to give good gifts to your children, how much more will your Father who is in heaven give good things to those who ask him?" (Matthew 7:11). Or to those who don't even know to ask!*

Thank you, God, (and Lynn!) for this gift named Winnie.

Misplaced Seating?

Changing gears a bit, let's look at the creative way God brought this next friend into my life. And don't miss the epilogue after the post, bringing you up to date on this friendship.

"The Woman on the Plane"

Day 381

I recently took a short trip over the one-year anniversary of Dale's death. Many of you saw the pictures on Facebook of the gorgeous scenery from Southern California. Such a blessing to enjoy that respite and to be rejuvenated during those days.

And obviously, the trip and the anniversary were essentially the "headlines" of the week. However, there was a subplot that took place before and after all the vacation hubbub.

When I select airline seats, I always choose the aisle if it's available. I like to be able to stand as soon as possible – and I don't usually like to feel hemmed in. As a kid, I loved the window seat, but I've moved on and don't have a strong desire to look at clouds for an extended period of time.

Yet, for some strange reason, when I boarded the plane in Des Moines for the first leg, I went and sat by the window. So, I got myself all belted in and said a cheery hello to the woman who came and took the middle seat; we'll call her "Middle Woman."

A few minutes later, another lovely lady stood by our row with a bit of a confused look on her face – and she was primarily looking at me! That's when I realized that, for some "unknown" reason, I had taken *her* window seat! So, we all reshuffled and settled back into our appropriate places. We'll name her "Window Woman." Kind of catchy, isn't it? Like Wonder Woman!

Shortly after that, Middle Woman says to Window Woman, "You look awfully familiar to me. Have we met?" And it turned out that they indeed had met. In fact, they both worked together some years ago in the healthcare industry.

That reconnection led to a lively conversation of catching up on their lives and their careers. I was now properly ensconced in the aisle seat, content to read my book for this multi-hour flight.

And then I heard it. Window Woman said that her husband, Bob, had passed away in May of this year and what a difficult time it was, both before and after his death. She mentioned how she had left her job to care for him as his health declined over the weeks preceding his death. And because her husband had been a pastor, she was not only grieving the loss of her husband, but also the hole left in the ministry they had together. And this trip was one that they traditionally took together.

While my first thought should have been, "Oh, I'm so sorry that you are walking this path," that's not what ran through my mind initially. It was this: "This is *not* a coincidence! God has put me on *this* flight in *this* row with *this* woman at *this* time!" Wow! Now what do I do with that?

Over the next two-plus hours, I did read some of the book, but also kept trying to half-listen for an opening in their conversation where I could jump in without looking totally rude. And I was praying that God would make it clear when to make that leap.

The obvious opening never came. The plane landed and I knew it was now or never. So, I lamely said to both of them, "So, is this your final destination?" I sounded like a flight attendant!! But they both answered in the affirmative and seemed to be very friendly towards me now as well.

So, I took the plunge and said to Window Woman, "I didn't intend to eavesdrop, but I couldn't help but hear about your husband's death. I'm so sorry for your loss. My husband died a year ago and I'm on a girlfriend trip to California because of that."

Oh goodness, the gates opened up for all three of us! And I don't mean the arrival gates! All three of us saw that this row placement was clearly from God's hand and we instantly and quickly exchanged contact information. I also gave Window Woman this blog address and told her to watch for the latest blog on the coming Tuesday. She promised to call me when she returned to Des Moines after her trip.

Then we all went our separate ways. For the time being.

She did, in fact, read and comment on that blog post, again promising to connect when she returned. And true to her word, she did call, and we talked for nearly an hour – and set up a time to get together over coffee to continue the conversation. Because if God so clearly brought us into each other's life, then we needed to see why!

During that conversation, she told me that her daughter had been praying that God would bring someone into her life *on that flight* who could be an encouragement to her. I get to use one of my favorite things – *Boom!*

If I had stayed quiet (I know, hard for me ...), Window Woman would have likely thought that the blessing her daughter prayed for was answered by the presence of Middle Woman. And it was definitely a blessing for both of them. But isn't it so like our God to give us even more than we can ask or imagine?

I don't know where this relationship will go, but we have a coffee date on our calendars, and we are both excited to get to know each other better and see where this journey takes us.

I continue to be amazed at the people God drops into my life during this season. It's one of the many ways he makes me feel so loved as he walks with me through this valley. I couldn't be more grateful for a God like that.

I hope this gives you a glimpse of his love, his grace, and his sovereignty. Three of my favorite "God qualities."

"Now to him who is able to do far more abundantly than all that we ask or think,according to the power at work within us,to him be glory in the church and in Christ Jesus throughout all generations, forever and ever. Amen."
Ephesians 3:20-21

Nearly a year and a half after this post, the "Window Woman" and I have had too many coffees and lunches to count, not to mention the hours we have spent on the phone together. We walk this widow journey together and have a depth of understanding for each other's grief that is unique and so precious. Chances are pretty good we are now life-long friends!

Who's a Writer?

Switching now from events that highlighted God's hand on my life, I want to emphasize a different avenue God has taken, but one that provided the same level of confirmation. It was experiencing how God choose to equip me for a ministry focused in large part on *writing*. Just a reminder that I have never considered myself a writer, other than for the annual Christmas letter. My background and interests have always been related to math and numbers. So here's a look at what this new experience looks like.

"My Writing Partner"

Day 586

One of the most amazing phenomena I've experienced in the past year or so can only be defined as God writing through me. I know how that must sound. Maybe a bit cheesy. Maybe a little too uber-spiritual. But it's a real and constant reminder to me of how little I contribute to this process.

This applies to the 36 blog posts I've written on this site beginning in February 2018, the 28 posts from the ministry site beginning last December, the three to four different speaking presentations I've written ... *and* a booklet I'm getting ready to self-publish. (Stay tuned for more on that!) I've even experienced this in my Christmas letters over the past couple of seasons, especially the one God wrote through me about a month after Dale's death.

Every time I sit down to write anything, I pray first and ask God to give me his words and to help me share the message that he wants in this ministry.

Oh sure, I usually come to my computer with a basic topic for a blog post and maybe what can only be described as an extremely skeletal outline. Usually it's a possible title and few random ideas (likely also from God ...).

Sometimes these topics have been rolling around in my head for a few weeks, and other times, the idea hits me completely out of the blue with an urgency that suggests I sit down and write *now*.

That's exactly what happened with this post. I was preparing to write something for the ministry site and, as always, prayed that prayer asking God to speak through me. And boom! This topic jumped out at me! It was essentially God telling me to share the joy and wonder of this writing miracle with my readers. Great idea, God!

So as soon as I scheduled the ministry post, I opened a new Word document – prayed – and then let God do what he has so faithfully done for so many months. He fills my mind and my soul with messages that always surprise me. He draws analogies for me. He leads me to scripture texts that perfectly illustrate his message. He even brings the best images for me to use weekly.

I don't struggle with what to say or how to say it. I don't have the infamous "writer's block." I just start to type, and the thoughts are almost always a few steps ahead of my fingers. It's one of the most astonishing things I've ever experienced.

So, for those of you who have so faithfully encouraged me with my writing, and extoled "my" writing skills, I do appreciate it and thank you for your kind words. But I want to stress again that it truly is not me. Yes, God may have given me some sort of command of the English language, but the result is his – and the ultimate praise and glory belong to him.

How can I adequately describe what this is like? I can tell you that I cry through almost everything I write. So, first of all, I'm generally exhausted when I'm done! But there is such a cleansing I feel through this process. It is truly my substitute for Christian counseling.

I am in awe whenever I finish writing. To know how little I have in my head when I sit down – and then to see God's finished product? I can think of few experiences that so clearly confirm God's power, his love for me, his hand on this ministry, and his involvement in the minute details of my life. I couldn't be more grateful or more astonished by it. And I just wanted you to know.

"You have said, 'Seek my face.' My heart says to you,
'Your face, Lord, do I seek.'"
Psalm 27:8

Writing update – Not only has God been the power behind all those personal and ministry blog posts, he has now added a couple of books to his list! It's astonishing … and humbling.

A New Writing Twist

My morning routine is quite predictable – read the local paper, do the Jumble and the crossword puzzle, read my devotions, and say a prayer for the day. All of this with one to three animals on my lap. On this particular morning, I had completed all of the above tasks and was just hanging out with the "kids" until I got the motivation to get on with my day.

And then it happened. The "random" thought from God was this, "I want you to write a CD of music." Are you kidding me?? Yes, I have been a musician since I started piano lessons with my mom at age six. I would consider myself classically trained. I don't play by ear; I don't make up songs; I just play what's written in the music.

So I ignored that prompting and got ready for the day. As I'm standing in the bathroom drying my hair, what do you suppose happened? God brought to my mind a title and words to a chorus. I felt like the music from *The Twilight Zone* should start playing. Yes, it gave me pause, but it did *not* make me obey God.

Next day, same thing. I'm doing my best to ignore all of this and God does it again. Gives me a title and words to a chorus. Do you ever wonder if God has a sense of humor? Well, here's proof. The title of this second song was, "Get Outta the Way." Yep, no kidding. It makes me laugh today, but I wasn't laughing back then.

But I *did* realize that God was calling me to another avenue in this ministry – song writing. So, I reluctantly sat down that evening with pencil and paper and waited for God to give me the words. Just a side note – I was used to God writing *words* through me, so I figured I'd start with that since God had already "proven" himself to me. But I'm *not* sitting down at the piano.

He did give me words to this first song, but when I did finally sit at the piano, the melody he placed in my head didn't exactly match those words. It's like he was saying to me, "Really? You couldn't trust me with *both* the words and the melody?" Sorry, God …

That first song was entitled "Thank You for Your Heart" and it was dedicated to the friends who have stuck by me through this journey. I guess God knows what he's doing, so I went to work on the second song, the funky "Get Outta the Way." Since then, we've also written, "I Long to See Your Face" which chronicles three ways this statement is true, and "Who Do You Trust" which challenges us to see why God is the only one who is trustworthy.

There are a couple more under construction with just titles and a few words, but given God's record (intentional pun) with this project, I'm confident there will be a full CD's worth in his timing.

I hope these stories illustrate what I experienced over and over these past few years. Happenings so completely "random" that they could only have come from the hand of God. I want these to encourage you and cause you to realize that God still moves in the lives of his children. I'm so grateful he's chosen to do so in mine.

I want to emphasize how much these "God sightings" have exploded in the days since Dale died. Again, I believe it's because he knows how desperately I need to see him in this season. But I can't help wonder how many sightings I've missed simply because I wasn't paying attention.

So this is my challenge to you – ask God to make his presence abundantly clear to you. And then wait expectantly for him to deliver. He wants to bless us, and experiencing his presence is *powerful*! He can and will show up in your life whether you are in a storm or in the sunshine. He's an all-weather God.

And so "the honest griever" is comforted by so clearly seeing God's hand upon her life.

SECTION V

Now What?

As we've explored throughout this book, we are completely different creatures after the loss of a spouse. Up to this point we have looked at much of the nitty-gritty of grieving and how that plays out in our new normal. Now we switch the focus from all that encompasses the reality of this new existence, and look at what lies ahead.

So, this final section will be looking into the future. Of course, not a future in the sense that I have any clue what it looks like, because only God is already there. But, in the sense that I want to examine what choices might be placed in front of me. And, to speculate as to what role I might take on as time passes, and as I continue to listen to God's leading for this new life he's given me. Finally, I'll combine a couple of concepts I've shared throughout this book. That of a forever grief, and the inevitability of joy and sorrow co-existing. How do those two concepts play out far into the future?

Maybe you're struggling with some of these same concepts. Perhaps you've already come to terms with some of the challenges presented. Likely you have some that I don't address. Regardless of what your list looks like, I hope the principles shared can help you move into your future, confident that a good God walks with you.

Whether spoken verbally or just in our heads, I think most of us must pose this question at some point, "Now what?"

18

God's Purpose in Widowhood

Deal First with Anger and Bitterness

I didn't always look for God's purpose through this pain. Deep down, I know that's what God wants, but sometimes I didn't want to admit that something this devastating could eventually have a godly purpose.

But gratefully, God didn't let me stay there often or for long. He was merciful enough to consistently drop those infamous "nuggets from heaven" into my daily despair. What about you? If you're struggling with those same emotions, how do you reach the point where you're *ready* to accept the fact that God can have a purpose through your loss?

One way is to see those blessings in the darkness. But you may have some other issues to deal with before you can land there. What if you're struggling with anger, or bitterness, or distrust of God? Those are prevalent emotions when someone has been dealt a major blow in their lives.

I believe you first must develop a desire to move past those destructive emotions. If you enjoy your misery, you will not be motivated to move past it. But as we'll discuss shortly, consider what that does to your witness.

I'm no psychiatrist, but I do know these difficult emotions must be addressed. Whether you go to a grief support group, or see a counselor, or talk it through with a trusted family member or friend, or write about it in blogs and books, as I do, it's crucial to reach a point where you begin to look for good things in your world, and see God for the good Father he is.

So, I'm going to assume for the remainder of this chapter that you've mostly reached that point. Then your heart will be open to the ways God wants to use us mightily in our season of loss.

Filling the "Husband Hole"

I've often described how I feel after Dale's death as having a "hole in my soul." There is an emptiness unlike anything I've ever experienced. I don't want to live with that hole, which I'll now rename the "Husband Hole." Kind of catchy, isn't it? Although, no one wants one of those! The same concept, of course, applies to widowers as well.

But the reality is that this emptiness seeps into many areas of our lives. Of course, the time we spent with our spouses, especially if they were sick towards the end of their lives, needs to be replaced with something. And I don't recommend pity parties being the hole filler.

In addition to the change in how you spend your time, you have also lost a crucial relationship which ideally must be replaced. (I'm not talking about husband or wife #2 here.) Our roles in the family, in our social circles, at church, and in almost every way you can imagine have now changed – or disappeared. Again, how do we replace those?

Our desires have also likely been shattered. Desire for a long marriage perhaps. Desire to travel. Desire to watch your children and grandchildren grow up together. Maybe even the desire to go *before* your spouse. I hear that a lot.

Recognizing this huge hole left by the loss of your spouse, regardless of the quality of your relationship, is a crucial step to take to allow God to use your heartache for your betterment and his glory.

But before we talk about how God wants to fill that hole, let's acknowledge that there are *many* other not-so-godly ways we try to fill up this hole. We can attempt to fill it with every kind of addiction that's out there from too much chocolate (my personal favorite) to alcohol, drugs, pity parties, over-spending, or even spouse-shopping. Guard your heart when it comes to the powerful force of "husband hole filling!"

Here's my challenge to you: why not fill this husband hole with a relationship we can never lose? Here's a little "teaser" from Carol Cornish's book, *The Undistracted Widow* explaining the beauty of how Christ is now our husband.

> "The church universal (all believers everywhere from all times) is the body of Christ and the bride of Christ. As his body

> and bride, Christ cherishes the church by lovingly caring for it. This care exercised in love is manifested collectively and individually. Christ lovingly cares for the church as a whole and each Christian as an individual part of his body and bride.
>
> "So, what does Christ's cherishing of his church mean for Christian widows? It means that Christ is now taking care of us directly without the mediating presence of a husband. The Lord will use means such as our church family, his Word, and so on, but we remain his direct concern. There is a sense in which Christ is now our husband, but we need to understand this truth carefully. This is not some silly, romance-novel idea.
>
> "The Bible uses many metaphors to communicate truth. A metaphor is the application of a representative word or phrase to somebody or something to make a comparison. Christ as husband means that Christ is concerned to perform the duties or a husband to his wife in the areas of protection and provision and even in some aspects of companionship."[11]

Isn't that a beautiful picture? Knowing how cherished I am by Christ, and how my protection and provision are now ultimately his responsibility is a comfort like no other.

Now, let's look at some additional scriptures and stories about widowhood.

God's Word Informs Us

Not to brag, but … we widows are often quite "front and center" in God's Word! Granted, it's likely none of us is looking for that kind of notoriety, but if this is our lot, it's important to understand the unique nature of our role in God's kingdom.

Let's look at the myriad of scriptures texts and stories where God addresses the widow, and discover what they tell us about God's heart for widows.

"Father to the fatherless and protector of widows
is God in His holy habitation" (Psalm 68:5).

"When Jesus saw his mother and the disciple whom
he loved standing nearby, he said to his mother,
'Woman, behold, your son!' Then he said to the disciple,
'Behold, your mother!' And from that hour the disciple
took her to his own home" (John 19:26-27).

"Religion that is pure and undefiled before God, the Father, is this: to visit orphans and widows in their affliction, and to keep oneself unstained from the world" (James 1:27).

"You shall not mistreat any widow or fatherless child. If you do mistreat them, and they cry out to me, I will surely hear their cry, and my wrath will burn, and I will kill you with the sword, and your wives shall become widows and your children fatherless" (Exodus 22:22-24).

"Learn to do good; seek justice, correct oppression; bring justice to the fatherless, plead the widow's cause" (Isaiah 1:17).

"The Lord tears down the house of the proud but maintains the widow's boundaries" (Proverbs 15:25).

"Honor widows who are truly widows. But if a widow has children or grandchildren, let them first learn to show godliness to their own household and to make some return to their parents, for this is pleasing in the sight of God. She who is truly a widow, left all alone, has set her hope on God and continues in supplications and prayers night and day" (I Timothy 5:3-5).

"For your maker is your husband – the Lord Almighty is his name" (Isaiah 54:5).

The story of the widow of Nain showcases Jesus' heart for this dear woman as we read in Luke 7:11-15.

> "Soon afterward he went to a town called Nain, and his disciples and a great crowd went with him. As he drew near to the gate of the town, behold, a man who had died was being carried out, the only son of his mother, and she was a widow, and a considerable crowd from the town was with her. And when the Lord saw her, he had compassion on her and said to her, 'Do not weep.' Then he came up and touched the bier, and the bearers stood still. And he said, 'Young man, I say to you, arise.' And the dead man sat up and began to speak, and Jesus gave him to his mother."

In addition to these texts, I can hardly exclude the heart-wrenching *and* heartwarming story in the book of Ruth. The short cliff notes version is this: Naomi is the mother-in-law of Ruth and Orpah and all three of them have lost their husbands recently and are now widows. Because of a famine in Naomi's native Judah, they were currently living in Moab.

After the death of her husband, Naomi planned to return to her homeland. Both daughters-in-law wanted to go with her and against Naomi's urging, Ruth insists on accompanying her beloved Naomi back to her home country. Eventually one of Naomi's kinsmen marries Ruth and it is primarily a happy ending. But there is loss and heartache woven throughout the story. In the end, what we remember most is loyalty, kindness, and redemption.

God's Heart for Widows

Are there certain themes that jump out at us as we read through these texts and stories? Do they reveal God's heart for widows? I believe God is incredibly clear. This is what they say to me about God's heart:

- God is our protector.
- Jesus has a heart for widows.
- God expects his people to honor widows.
- God becomes our husband.
- The church is called to demonstrate her faith by caring for widows.

Clearly, the widow of the scriptures rises to the top of the hierarchy of church responsibilities. Why do you suppose that is true? I believe it's a reflection of all I wrote about in Chapter 12 – Widow Grief. It's a pain like no other and God understands the need for extraordinary care for the widow. To put himself in the place of my husband is powerful and humbling. Just another gospel truth that I struggle to fully grasp.

When you see the compassionate heart God has for the widow and combine that with God's desire to *always* bring good out of heartache, is it any wonder that he would give the widow purpose in her widowhood?

While my perspective is obviously that of a widow, I believe that many of the concepts we'll look at can be applied to widowers as well, or to anyone experiencing a deep loss. Adjust as necessary!

God's Unique Purpose

So, let's take a practical look at what it means to be a widow in this world. We are now completely different people. There is no "us" anymore. There is no couple. There is no "till death do us part" relationship. In so many ways, our world has been turned upside down. It's still full of heartache. And yet, for me personally, I don't want my life to be defined by those difficulties. I *need* to break through the heartbreak and find a new purpose for my life.

The desire to be useful, in general, and used of God, specifically, is so prevalent in the lives of widows I know. We want to find some meaning in this new life. What do we bring to the table? What characteristics of our widowhood can be a blessing to others?

What this looks like will be as varied as the personalities of the widows. Even though we have our widowhood in common, our gifts and talents and desires continue to be unique. And finding that unique "slot" into which we now fit is a task worth tackling.

Lots of factors will affect where we land in that quest. There's a huge difference between the 30-year-old widow who is still raising children at home, and the 90-year-old widow who is living in a care facility. So there's obviously no "one-size-fits-all" solution to finding a purpose.

The young widowed mother will likely be overwhelmed with the realities of raising her family alone. *That* is highly likely her purpose now. Sure, it was her job before her husband died, but now she is filling the role of both parents and that just elevated her purpose.

The elderly widow may be in her last days and limited by physical and/or mental constraints. Perhaps her purpose is now lending a listening ear, or becoming a more dedicated prayer warrior, or knitting scarves for her great grandchildren!

The "what" doesn't matter as much as the choosing of the "what." As we discussed earlier, the hole left in our lives by our spouses' deaths just begs for something to fill it. It may take time to find your new rhythm. Family or job responsibilities may leave little room for other new adventures, but I still believe it's essential to add something that can satisfy that part of your soul that lost so much.

What Can We Bring to the Table?

Do we really have much to offer this world? Sometimes it feels like all we do is take from others, especially in those early days. We can be extremely needy for a long time! And, healing must often break through the sorrow before we have the energy to contribute to society.

Let's think about the ways widowhood has molded us into women who have unique perspectives we can share with those around us.

- We know the importance and power of compassion.
- We now have a boatload of empathy for those who are suffering.
- We have learned that it's critical to appreciate what we have in our lives.
- We have learned what it means to rely on God's strength.
- We've [mostly] survived the most devastating loss of our lives.
- God may have opened our eyes to new scripture revelations.
- We have lessons to share that only widowhood can teach.
- We may have more time to devote to important causes.

- We may have more time for grandkids.
- We can have a single-minded focus on God's kingdom.

Do you see how incredible these skills and experiences are? How hungry the world is for the things we can offer? Please don't sell yourself short. Maybe your new world of widowhood is completely consumed by caring for your young children. That doesn't mean you can't infuse your new-found wisdom into the lives of others, even if it's short conversation snippets with other moms.

Maybe you have virtually no obligations now that your husband is gone. You have the opportunity to jump into God's purpose with both feet, if you so desire.

No matter how much time or energy you have to give, ask God to show you the ways he wants to bless others through your wisdom and perspectives. Just as God finds purpose in every pain we experience, so will he give us purpose through our widowhood. He is your Husband, and he will lead you through this season and into a greater responsibility that only *you* can fulfill.

The Ultimate Purpose

I suspect that many readers are familiar with the biblical passage best known as "The Great Commission." It was Jesus' final words to his disciples, and to all of us, before he returned to his Father and the glory of heaven.

> "Go therefore and make disciples of all nations, baptizing them in the name of the Father and of the Son and of the Holy Spirit, teaching them to observe all that I have commanded you. And behold, I am with you always, to the end of the age" (Matthew 28:19-20).

"What if I'm not an evangelist or a missionary?" you may ask. Most of us aren't, at least not in any official capacity. But the commandment is still aimed at us, even us widows or widowers. So which part of this commandment might we step into? How about the "making disciples" part?

We often hear people say, as Christians, we may be the only Bible that people will ever read. In other words, the way we live our lives can have a powerful influence on someone's path to Jesus. What better opportunity to live a life of impact than to let others see how God's character and promises are reflected in how we respond to this devastating blow to our world?

Do we hang onto our anger at God? Have we stepped out of the world and into our cocoon because we haven't tapped into God's healing power? Do we constantly question why God would "punish" us this way? Do we refuse to experience joy or see any of God's blessings in our life?

Or do we acknowledge his goodness despite our trial? Do we run to him first when we need to pour out our hearts of pain? Do we consciously look for, and be grateful for, the blessings he bestows on us? Do we turn the control of our lives over to him and allow him to mold us through this fire? Do we know, beyond a shadow of a doubt, that he *does* have a purpose for us through this pain.

What an incredibly unique position we are in as Christian widow(er)s. If we can see the *Son* through our rainy days, our witness to an unbelieving world will be *powerful*! That's what I want the rest of my life to be. No matter what road God takes me down, I want my pain – and my reaction to it – to be the light that draws others to me to ask, "What's different about you? How can you be joyful through this?"

"Let me tell you how …"

And so "the honest griever" begins to understand how God can use her through this season.

19

To Marry or Not to Marry

That is the question. It's a question that was posed to me even *before* Dale passed away. Not by complete strangers, mind you, but close friends have asked me if I thought I would get married after Dale was gone. They knew he was 20 years older and I was highly likely to outlive him. So I wasn't offended by the question. My answer then and my answer now is the same. "It's not my call."

The Bottom Lines

That's the most important bottom line for this chapter. I don't know the mind of God, and I can't anticipate what he might have planned for me two weeks from now or ten years from now. So before I get into all the "marriage analysis," I want you to remember this. Ultimately, this question is answered by God.

We just left a chapter that delineated all the wonderful reasons that Christ is now our Husband after our earthly husbands have died. Those benefits are still 100% true regardless of any future marriage plans. So that's another bottom line I'd like you to remember. Having Christ as our Husband doesn't prevent you from marrying another human being someday.

And finally, regardless of where I currently stand on this issue, I promise to look at it from all sides … eventually!

Where I Stand

So with those concepts firmly in place, I can now tell you how I feel about this whole remarriage topic! The statement I make right after the "It's not my call" declaration is this, "I can't imagine starting over with someone else."

I need you to know where I personally have landed on this issue, for now, and then we'll get into the other issues affecting this decision.

If you haven't noticed already, let me make it abundantly clear. Dale and I had a love unlike anything either one had experienced before. I've been in love with him most of my adult life, and still am. I will unabashedly use clichés such as "soul mate" and "love of my life" because he was all that to me and more.

Even the idea of dating is completely foreign to me, so the whole marriage thing is so far out of my land of possibilities that it isn't even a question. I have turned down dates because of this.

Do I have friends who would like me to start dating? Sure. They know how lonely I am and feel that a companion would be the perfect solution to that. Their hearts are in the right place. I don't fault them for it.

I'm still wearing my wedding ring that Dale picked out in 1985. I'm not ready to take it off, and after about the two-year mark, I stopped fretting over what the right time might be to make that decision. Here's a blog post that gives you a little more insight into this world.

"The Wedding Ring"

Day 550

I'm a big fan of the show, *Blue Bloods*. Maybe it's because I've also always been a fan of Tom Selleck from back in the *Magnum P.I.* days. But I've come to appreciate every character on the show over the past few years.

So, you can usually find me curled up on the couch with two or three animals every Friday night at 9:00 p.m. watching the professional and personal interactions of the Reagan family dynasty. (Yes, we widows lead exciting lives ...)

Detective Danny Reagan, one of Frank's (Tom Selleck) sons, lost his wife tragically on the show a while back. So, he is now a single dad trying to raise two teenaged boys. Sometimes he's successful, sometimes not so much. But through it all, he is clearly heart-broken over the loss of his sweet and sassy RN wife, Linda.

So, there are episodes that take Danny through some of his grief that are hard for me to watch – and I relate to the pain and loss he is experiencing.

But I was *not* prepared for a portion of the show this past Friday night. Linda has been gone for over a year and Danny is still wearing his wedding ring. I completely relate to that. I still wear my wedding ring, in part because I still feel like I'm married to Dale even though he's been gone 18 months this week.

In this scene, Danny has gone to visit a woman who is some sort of psychic or counselor or combination thereof. She comments on the fact that he still wears his ring. He looks a bit sheepish as he acknowledges that fact. She then "reminds" him that Linda is gone now. (*Really*? Do you think he's not aware?) Then she tells him it's time to stop wearing it.

She brings a little velvet jewelry pouch over and he gently removes the ring and drops it in the pouch. I burst into tears! Where did that come from? I was *so* unprepared for that reaction – and for the visceral, immediate nature of it.

In a split second, I experienced what I assumed Danny was feeling – the physical, visual acknowledgment that his marriage and relationship were over. It hit me like a ton of bricks, like the body slam that it was. I couldn't stop crying. Just one more reminder that this grieving process can go on and on and on ... a forever grief.

So, where do I stand on this whole wedding ring removal issue? Clearly, I'm not ready to take the step Danny took! I do know that Dale's gone, that he's not coming back. I now mark "widowed" on any forms I must fill out. I do know that my marriage is over. There's no disillusionment there. I'm reminded every moment of every day that he's not here anymore.

And yet, I can*not* bring myself to take that step. I know that I probably will ... someday. But today isn't that day. I know some people remove it as soon as their loved one dies; and I know some who still wear their ring, on their left hand, 30-some years after their husband died.

As with everything in this grieving process, it's our call. Unlike the "psychic-counselor" of *Blue Bloods*, I don't want anyone to tell me when it's time. It's a very personal decision and even I have no idea when "it's time." I trust that God will let me know the if and when.

"Therefore a man shall leave his father and mother and hold fast to his wife, and the two shall become one flesh."
Ephesians 5:31

Who Decides My Best Life?

Let me address one more issue on this subject that I deal with regularly, and explain why it's become a bit of a challenge for me lately. Possibly some new "food for thought" for my readers. Please hear my heart that wants to educate and enlighten, and not criticize.

Often when the subject of dating or remarriage comes up in a conversation with friends, and I give my pat answers (Not my call, Can't imagine starting over), the friend will be quick to add, "Well, of course you know God could bring someone into your life." Yes, I'm aware. And if God whacks me over the head to get my attention on this issue, I promise to listen.

Obviously, they feel that the happier outcome for my life would be to find someone to love again and get remarried. Well, here's the thing. What makes them so sure that remarriage is the best option for me? How do they know that remarriage is what God wants for my life? Isn't it possible that God has other plans to use me that don't involve a husband?

Because society is so couple-driven, it's hard for many to accept the idea that being single, or staying single is a good option for anyone. So to balance the clear bias from society, I'd like to highlight some biblical reasons and supporting scripture texts that give credence to the single life.

Before I share specific scriptures, let me say that my identity doesn't rest in whether I have a husband or not. Yes, it was a huge part of who I was for over 30 years, but that's over. My worth and my identity are found in who I am in Christ. This isn't some women's lib mantra from the 70s and 80s. I'm not declaring that I'm strong enough to never need a man in my life. I'm simply putting the proper perspective on how we can live fulfilled, godly lives without a husband.

A Biblical View of Both Options

Now let's see what God's Word says about staying single, or not remarrying.

"I want you to be free from anxieties. The unmarried man is anxious about the things of the Lord, how to please the Lord. But the married man is anxious about worldly things, how to please his wife, and his interests are divided. And the unmarried or betrothed woman is anxious about the things of the Lord, how to be holy in body and spirit. But the married woman is anxious about worldly things, how to please her husband. I say this for your own benefit, not to lay any restraint upon you, but to promote good order and to secure your undivided devotion to the Lord" (1 Corinthians 7:32-35).

"To the unmarried and the widows I say that it is good for them to remain single as I [Paul] am" (1 Corinthians 7:8).

"For when they rise from the dead, they neither marry nor are given in marriage, but are like angels in heaven" (Mark 12:25).

The main message from these verses is this – if a man or a woman remains single, their devotion to God will have fewer distractions than if they have a spouse and/or a family that needs and deserves their attention.

If I was into "name dropping," I might mention that two of the most important figures in the New Testament, Jesus and the Apostle Paul, were single! I'm only half kidding. It's an honorable position to take and we singles are in decent company.

Most of the scripture texts that show strong support for marriage refer primarily to younger people and likely first marriages. Of course, in Genesis we know that God says, "It is not good for man to be alone." So we know that the original plan included marriage. God's command to "be fruitful and multiply" is best obeyed within the confines of marriage.

There is also sufficient support for singles and widow(er)s to marry if they cannot control their desires. As Paul says in 1 Corinthians 7:9, "But if they cannot exercise self-control, they should marry. For it is better to marry than to burn with passion."

The Bible is clear on one point. "A wife is bound to her husband as long as he lives. But if her husband dies, she is free to be married to whom she wishes, ***only in the Lord***" (1 Corinthians 7:39). Do not marry an unbeliever, no exceptions.

We talked earlier about the wide range of circumstances in which widows find themselves – from the 30-year-old young mom to the 90-year-old care facility resident. Certainly, the young mother may long for a mate to help raise her family and be her companion for the long life that she hopes is ahead of her. And conversely, the elderly widow may be looking forward to a reunion with her husband in heaven.

That said, don't we all know exceptions to those stereotypes? I know women who lost their husbands when they were in their prime and never remarried. And I believe we all smile a bit when we see stories of two elderly people who have fallen in love and married well into their 80s.

Which brings me full circle to my earlier statement. It's not our call.

Dangerous Reasons to Remarry

Are there wrong reasons to get remarried? No question. Just as there are wrong reasons to marry in our youth, there are wrong reasons to remarry as widows and widowers. Let's lay out a few of them.

- **I'm lonely**. This is a tough one because loneliness is such an integral part of our lives as widows and widowers. I'd put both emotional and physical loneliness in this category because either or both can have a strong pull into remarriage. But it's critical for us to reach a point where we've learned to live with this loneliness, and have instead turned to God for comfort. Striving for a life of service to others is a wonderful remedy for loneliness. Don't make loneliness the only reason you remarry.
- **I need a handyman/accountant/mechanic/cook/housekeeper/nurse**. If we're just looking for a mate to take over certain household chores, then we're better off learning the skill ourselves, asking a friend or family member to help us, or paying a professional. None of us wants to feel like we're filling a job opening.
- **I need financial support.** It seems that I'm stating the obvious here, but what kind of foundation do you build on if you're marrying for money? Fond memory rabbit trail - During my high school and college years, my dad used to say to me, "Don't marry for money, but learn to love a guy who's got it!" Oh dad, you and your sense of humor. But this is a foundation built on sand.
- **I need a father/mother for my children**. That may very well be true, and will likely be a major factor in choosing a mate for a young widow(er). But that can't be enough. You must both feel God's leading to enter into this marriage, or the challenges of child-rearing could overwhelm your commitment to each other.
- **This person is a Christian**. That's great, but is it enough? No way. Yes, make it the leading criterion, but don't make it the *only* criterion.
- **He/she reminds me so much of my husband/wife**. Oh goodness, this is a recipe for disaster! One of the reasons I can't imagine remarrying is because I think I would constantly be comparing the person to

Dale. And they would never measure up. What an injustice is done to this new spouse if your expectation is for them to step into your dead spouse's shoes.

- **This might be my only chance.** Can you say, "desperate?" Does anyone think that's a solid reason to begin another "till death do us part" relationship? And honestly, how do you know that? If God wants you to find a mate, he will bring him or her to you. No desperation needed.
- **He or she gets along with my children/parents/friends/pets.** It's lovely that you've found someone who fits in with your current family and social circles. Be friends on Facebook perhaps, but don't marry just for that reason.

Circumstances are so varied here that I know there are dozens more bad reasons to get married. It feels like a mine field, doesn't it? Add to this, the unique challenges we face today with social media and on-line dating and the associated facades that disguise who the person *really* is. No wonder it's best for God to do this work for us!

If I'm honest (as the book title says I must be), most of the time the whole process feels like too much work! I don't want to start over at this stage of my life.

And then I remind myself, "It's not my call!" So I end this chapter still feeling zero desire to remarry, but with a mind and heart open to whatever God might bring to me down the road. And a prayer that I would be content taking either fork in that road.

That is my advice to you as well. If God is clearly calling you to remarry another believer, then rejoice in the gift he's brought to you.

And so "the honest griever" finds contentment in her "singleness."

20

Future Sorrow

Is That Biblical?

You may be thinking, "Enough with the sorrow already!" I couldn't agree more. I'd join the billions of people who'd prefer no more sorrow in their lives. Of course, that's not the reality in which we reside, is it?

So just what is "future sorrow?" Doesn't the Bible warn us against this kind of thinking? "Sufficient for the day is its own trouble" (Matthew 6:34b). I'm not encouraging anyone, myself included, to spend our days worrying about how hard – or sorrowful – tomorrow might be.

What I am encouraging, however, is an honest expectation of what lies ahead for those of us who have suffered a life-altering loss. As we well know, grief isn't a light switch that you can turn on and off. If it were, we'd leave it in the "off" position permanently.

In this chapter, I want to explore what sorrow will likely remain in my life throughout my years, and what pitfalls we all need to be watchful of, so that we don't sink too low into that pit. I believe that's simply good self-care for anyone, regardless of what kinds of losses you've encountered.

With only 30 months of "rearview mirror" experience with this sorrow, I don't have a broad base upon which to draw the expectations for the rest of my life. But I've seen enough changes in my grief, and learned enough lessons – mostly the hard way – to speak with some authority on this subject.

Grief Morphs

I can attest to the changing nature of grief from the moment of Dale's death pronouncement until today. We covered much of that in the whole section on grief, so I won't revisit much of that. Even examining the differences between years one and two of widowhood shed some light on this morphing process. And if you recall, there wasn't improvement between those years, but rather a worsening of the sorrow.

So, this morphing that we'll talk through is certainly not a straight-line graph. With all the complexities of grief, there are multiple measurements one could take. Let me illustrate with this story. I often find friends and acquaintances sincerely wanting my grief to be significantly less today than it was 30 months ago. I appreciate the sentiment. But, it's not that simple. My recent response to them is always, "Well, I'm not curled up in a fetal position on the bathroom floor anymore, but I have now been sad for *x* months and that has a noticeable, cumulative effect on a person."

This does elicit a few confused looks on their faces, but I believe the point is well made. I can't state that my grief now is *better* than it was right after Dale died. I can only say it is different. And based on all the ways I've experienced those changes, I can only assume it will continue to morph well into the future, and maybe into forever.

Do I expect it to get better? In some ways, yes, in some ways, no. I'll mention again my widow friend who told me she is lonelier now than she was eight years ago when her husband died, because she has now been without him longer. I completely get that.

The key, I believe, is to temper our expectations of what grief will become. If we think we can reach a predetermined anniversary and find that all is now well, we will be sorely disappointed. Because I've learned so much through this journey, I can only expect that to continue. As my grief changes, I will look for the lessons. I will look to God to continue walking by my side through whatever my grief becomes in the years ahead.

At the risk of sounding pitiful, I do expect to always have this "hole in my soul." I do believe *this* loss is my forever grief. I hope you've learned by this point in the book that it's only one facet of how I view my life. Stay tuned for the next chapter!

Beware the Deceiver

As I examine some of the struggles we are most likely to face, let me share a word of warning. Satan, the Father of Lies, wants nothing more than to attack you wherever you're most vulnerable and subsequently try to destroy your witness to the world.

If you doubt his power, look at these verses from the Bible.

> "Be sober-minded; be watchful. Your adversary the devil prowls around like a roaring lion, seeking someone to devour" (1 Peter 5:8).

> "You are of your father the devil, and your will is to do your father's desires. He was a murderer from the beginning, and has nothing to do with the truth, because there is no truth in him. When he lies, he speaks out of his own character, for he is a liar and the father of lies" (John 8:44).

> "And no wonder, for even Satan disguises himself as an angel of light" (2 Corinthians 11:14).

> "Submit yourselves therefore to God. Resist the devil, and he will flee from you" (James 4:7).

> "Put on the whole armor of God, that you may be able to stand against the schemes of the devil" (Ephesians 6:11).

This is a small sampling, but the point is clear. Satan only wants destruction for us, and he knows how and when to attack to be most effective. Don't let him get a foothold in your life. Put on the full armor of God that the Apostle Paul talks about in Ephesians, Chapter 6.

Be watchful. Ask God to protect you. If you slip, ask God to restore you. Greater is he that is in me than he that is in the world. Ultimately, Satan is a defeated foe. Trust God for that.

Future Fears

Since the loss of a spouse makes the top spot in most "Stressful Circumstances" lists, it's understandable that fear can accompany your long-term outlook. I wish it could be as simple as telling you, "Don't be afraid." The word "fear" shows up in the ESV version of the Bible 437 times! Of course, some of those times are telling us to fear the Lord (in the awe-inspiring way), but so many of them are encouraging us time and time again to put our trust in this sovereign God. Do you think the Bible would need to remind us that often if it weren't something so many struggle with? God understands our frailty here.

I'll list some of my favorite verses in a bit, but first want to acknowledge the fact that our fears about the future can seem limitless. How will I survive emotionally? Will I need to move? How can I live alone? Who will take care of me when I'm sick? How long will my money last? Who can I turn to for household chores? Will I lose my friends? What if I can't find purpose in my life? Will I ever heal?

Oh goodness, so many ways to be fearful. So, I don't want to minimize that reality. Yes, there can be no end to the fears and "what ifs" that flood our souls, especially at night when it's so hard to turn our brains off! Of course, nighttime is when Satan does some of his best work.

The most effective way I've found to counter those fears, and figuratively spit in Satan's face, is to meditate on the scriptures that give us reason to turn it all over to God. Here's my promised list of favorites.

"Fear not, for I am with you; be not dismayed, for I am your God; I will strengthen you, I will help you, I will uphold you with my righteous right hand" (Isaiah 41:10).

"When I am afraid, I put my trust in you" (Psalm 56:3).

"Have I not commanded you? Be strong and courageous. Do not be frightened, and do not be dismayed, for the Lord your God is with you wherever you go" (Joshua 1:9).

"Do not be anxious about anything, but in everything by prayer and supplication with thanksgiving let your requests be made known to God. And the peace of God, which surpasses all understanding, will guard your hearts and your minds in Christ Jesus" (Philippians 4:6-7).

"The Lord is on my side; I will not fear. What can man do to me?" (Psalm 118:6).

"There is no fear in love, but perfect love casts out fear. For fear has to do with punishment, and whoever fears has not been perfected in love" (1 John 4:18).

"Even though I walk through the valley of the shadow of death, I will fear no evil, for you are with me; your rod and your staff, they comfort me" (Psalm 23:4).

"Casting all your anxieties on him, because he cares for you" (1 Peter 5:7).

"For God gave us a spirit not of fear but of power and love and self-control" (2 Timothy 1:7).

"The Lord is my light and my salvation; whom shall I fear? The Lord is the stronghold of my life; of whom shall I be afraid?" (Psalm 27:1).

"Be strong and courageous. Do not fear or be in dread of them, for it is the Lord your God who goes with you. He will not leave you or forsake you" (Deuteronomy 31:6).

"I sought the Lord, and he answered me and delivered me from all my fears" (Psalm 34:4).

Not a bad list, is it? This is where you rest when fear threatens to consume you. There is power in God's Word. It's written for you and for me.

Still the Memories

We've seen throughout this book how so much of what we grieve stays with us, to some degree, throughout our lives. Memories are no different. The impact they have on our emotions can change through the years, but the memories remain. And that is my prayer. I don't want to lose the memories I shared with Dale. It's one of the best ways I stay connected to him and the life we lived together.

But inherent in those memories is the opportunity for continued sorrow. It's a package deal. I wouldn't trade the heartwarming effect they have on my life with the opportunity to ignore them and any associated pain. It's one of the many new realities of widowhood that I've had to accept. Here we go again – sorrow and joy co-existing.

So I would not discourage anyone from enjoying those uplifting thoughts, even with the little heart stabs they bring. But I would caution against *looking* for memories that can make you sad or tearful. Maybe that's appropriate on a special anniversary date, but ultimately flooding your heart and mind with these difficult memories intentionally, may do more harm than good. The result can be a downward slide into a prolonged pity party which isn't helpful and isn't what God wants for our lives.

Quite frankly, I don't need to go looking for a memory. They pop into my head regularly and I can choose to saturate myself with the heartache, or take a moment to reflect and then move on.

Case in point, every other morning as I make a slice of peanut butter toast for breakfast, I'm reminded without fail of Dale. He was notorious for his fanaticism about the proper way to butter toast. It was not done properly unless the butter reached the far edges all around the slice. Seems reasonable until you see if you abide by that rule!

As much as I *love* butter, I found that I did *not* adhere to this principle initially. It did not take long, however, before I was a devotee to the idea as well. My mom was so afraid she wouldn't live up to Dale's toast-buttering expectations that she wouldn't ever make him toast!

So every other morning at the kitchen counter, I smile when I think about his passion for toast-buttering.

Dissatisfaction with Your Life

Another sorrow, of sorts, is being so unhappy with how your life turned out, that you can't see any of the good God wants to bring from it. Whether you lost a spouse or a loved one unexpectedly at an early age, or saw the death coming for years towards the end of your life, it's challenging not to want that old life back again. Sadly, we are surrounded by reminders of what we've lost and rising above that self-pity can be difficult. God forced me to look at how I had fallen into that bad habit as well. Here's the blog post where I examine my shortcomings in this area.

"I Want What You Have!"

Day 715

On a very regular basis, I tell Daisy, "You can't have all the bones! You have to share with Winnie." As you can see in the picture, she has three of the four in her pile. And she had just been scolded for trying to take the last one from Winnie. This is a daily occurrence at my house.

I want to get frustrated with Daisy because she *never learns* that she doesn't get to have *everything*. And specifically – whatever her sister might have. Although I must admit, this routine does provide a certain bit of entertainment for me!

Even though I wonder why Daisy can't quite understand this concept after so many years of correction, I had to stop and ask myself the very same question. How often have I said (mostly to myself), "I want what you have?"

In this season of widowhood and the few years leading up to it, where my life changed drastically, I find myself longing for the things others still have. They still have a husband; they still go on vacations with him; they still have holiday gatherings with their family; they still go out for Valentine's Day; they still have someone to process their day with; they still have someone to share their highs and lows with. I could go on and on.

So, I admit to wanting these things that others have. Seriously, I'm no better than Daisy!

I need a constant reminder, it seems, to remember that the life I'm living right now is *exactly* the life God has planned for me. I'm fully aware of the inevitability of trials in our lives – some minor, some devastating. It's part of the fabric of life in this fallen world.

Clearly, I've seen God work through my trials – and have written about that often. So the fact that my "go-to" response continues to be, "I want what you have" means my thinking needs tweaking once again! Seems I'm doing that a lot lately ...

Here's where I'm trying to focus: I'm grateful for the life God gave me with Dale. I'm grateful for the blessings he continues to bestow on me even now. I'm grateful for the people in my life who lift me up when I'm down. I'm beyond grateful to be a child of God who is loved beyond measure. And I'm eternally grateful for the hope of heaven through Jesus' sacrifice on the cross.

What about you? Do you want what others have? If you do, I'd say you're in good company! However, I'd encourage you to look at how your life has been blessed. Or look to see how God wants to refine you and yes, improve you, through your difficulties.

We only get one shot at this earthly life. Don't waste time and energy wishing you had what others have. Embrace the life God has given you – and be content with one or two bones!

"I know how to be brought low, and I know
how to abound. In any and every circumstance,
I have learned the secret of facing
plenty and hunger, abundance and need."
Philippians 4:12

Finding Balance

This must be one of the most difficult struggles of widow(er)hood. Finding the proper balance in virtually every aspect of our lives. Balancing joy and sorrow. Balancing social activities with loneliness. Heartache with blessings. Fear with trust. Pity parties with self-care. Anger with acceptance. Bitterness with gratitude. The present with the future. So many ways we must juggle the emotions of this season.

I rarely get it all right. Best I can do is find a happy medium in a category or two. This next post asks us all that question.

"How Is Your Life Balance?"

Day 254

Who *isn't* trying to find some balance in their lives nowadays? I think our schedule-crazy society works against nearly everyone, including kids. I'm blown away by all the options available to the kiddos and secretly wish they didn't have so many. I loved my carefree childhood days where the only commitments I had were swimming lessons for a few weeks and Vacation Bible School. Ahhh, the good old days … (said June Cleaver!)

The balance I want to chat about in this post, however, isn't that issue. It's an idea that came to me after my prayer time this morning.

I continue to struggle with sadness every day, and the 20-plus months of that since Dale's death is absolutely exhausting. I'm also coming to grips with the fact that this is very much the reality of my life now and probably will be for an awfully long time. Hard not to focus on that when it permeates my soul daily.

So to combat that, I decided to change that focus to the ever-popular "attitude of gratitude." Or, in other words, change the balance in my life. I've taken multiple stabs at that in the past year or two, but it doesn't always stick.

I did begin to thank God for the blessings that are ever-present in my life today. I thanked him for the blessed life I had for so very many years. And I am immeasurably excited about and grateful for what lies ahead in an eternity in heaven.

So, the statistician in me took over the analysis at this point. (For those of you who haven't heard; a statistician is someone with their head in the oven and their feet in ice water who says, "On average, I feel fine." Sorry, I couldn't resist that. I have so few opportunities to use math humor ...)

Back to the subject at hand. When I thought about how much of my past has been good and added to that the parts of my present that are good and added to that the future that will be *amazing*, guess what conclusion I came to? When eternity is part of that equation, there is barely a sliver of time that is anything but good! It must be something like 99.99999999999 ... % incredible! How's that for a new focus?

Even if your life on this earth has been full of trials and difficulties, if you know that heaven is your future home, you too will have virtually no bad times showing up in your life balance scales.

An eternity of perfection wipes away *any* difficulties we've experienced in this life, no matter how plentiful they are.

Of course, it doesn't feel like that when we're in the middle of this present world. Only in retrospect will we come to fully understand and enjoy this glorious truth.

But it did help me to look at my pain a bit differently. Less permanent, less all-encompassing, less discouraging, less heart-wrenching. It reminded me to keep fighting the good fight. Keep focusing on God's will in my life. Keep counting my blessings. And keep my eyes on "Jesus, the author and perfecter of my faith" (Hebrews 12:2).

So, how is your life balance? Would it help to have an eternal perspective? Could you ask God to help you develop it? I'm pretty sure it's what would honor him the most. It will be my prayer for you.

"For this light momentary affliction is preparing for us an eternal weight of glory beyond all comparison ..."
2 Corinthians 17:14

"What is your life? For you are a mist that appears for a little time and then vanishes."
James 4:14

So to recap and wrap up this chapter, future sorrow isn't about expecting nothing but heartache for the rest of our lives. It's about realistically acknowledging that challenges will follow us into the future. We are wise to watch out for the devil's arrows, and trust *daily* in a God who wants to be our constant companion.

And so "the honest griever" takes a candid look at what heartache lies ahead.

21

Future Joy

How encouraging to sit and imagine what joy God might have in store for us in the years ahead. As in the last chapter, I don't have a crystal ball to know what future sorrow or future joy will look like, but I base some of my speculation on what I've experienced over the past few years. Without a doubt, imagining future joy, even in those first hard days, is what keeps me going, and gets me out of bed in the morning.

We talked about the co-existence of joy and sorrow in our present world. But I believe the same concept is true for our future. To balance the future sorrow we just outlined, let's take a look at the encouragement of future joy.

What Will Your Purpose Become?

We talked in Chapter 18 about finding a purpose through widowhood, or more correctly, allowing God to lead you into the work he wants you to do going forward. If he's made that clear to you, then you have a jump start on joy.

As we know, God doesn't always reveal that plan on our schedule, so until you feel that you've landed on the bullseye, you may be on a few detours. And honestly, not everyone finds an obvious purpose for their widow(er)hood or their season of loss. If that describes you, it doesn't mean you can't find joy in *some* purpose. There are so many opportunities to spread kindness and compassion and yes, joy, that I encourage you to step through any door that leads to those kinds of openings.

If you do feel God's call upon your life, then embrace it! It may be a full-time ministry or a shift in focus in the job you already have. Maybe it's a prayer ministry or working with others who have gone through losses. The possibilities are endless. Perhaps God leads you to it in the first few weeks after your loss or maybe it only becomes clear many years down the road.

The important thing is to be open to God's leading and to hold your own expectations lightly. Let God surprise you with his plan like he did with me. He's a creative God and may have bigger plans for you than you would have for yourself. Or he will show you how to have an impact even through the mundane pieces of your life.

I shared with you how God led me to a ministry that was the direct result of Dale's death. It's not what I would have chosen for myself, but in retrospect, I see that it is the perfect fit for my life today. It uses everything I've learned through my lifetime and applies it to his purpose today. The passion I feel for my subject matter is greater by far than anything I've experienced in my life. God has clearly given me "the desires of my heart." And the bonus for me is that he continues to confirm this calling with every single step I take, not the least of which is this book!

To say I'm grateful doesn't begin to capture what this means to me. I'm in awe almost daily to see how he guides me and gives me words to say and write. To see the doors he opens where I least expect them. To see the people he has brought into my life to help me with this ministry.

Every piece of this ministry isn't smooth sailing, mind you, but even in those times of struggle, I knew he walked beside me and eventually brought me out of whatever hole I had fallen into. It's a partnership I wouldn't trade for anything.

If you're reading this book, you are part of my ministry and I'm so thankful you've chosen to learn from my lessons. So, look expectantly to the future, knowing that God is already there and knows exactly the joy he has planned for you.

Personal Growth and Sharing Life Lessons

Any chance you've learned everything God wants you to know about this life? Nope. Me neither. Think with me a moment about just one lesson you've learned since you suffered your loss. Was it earth-shattering? Was it a gentle reminder? Or somewhere in between? I've learned scores of lessons, often quite reluctantly, but with eventual great impact.

If you have even one example that gave you some joy through that revelation or experience, then you know what is likely in your future. God *wants* to continue imparting his wisdom to us until our days on this earth are over.

The knowledge any one of us has right now about God is barely the tip of the iceberg of all that is still undiscovered.

Can you imagine a future that continues to enlighten us with more and more revelations of God's character and his promises? I listed just a small sampling of those in Chapter 14 and that barely scratched the surface of God's attributes. The amount of knowledge to be gained, and the associated joy at those revelations, is truly mind-boggling. There is more than enough to fill a million lifetimes.

So, how do we capitalize on our personal growth and lessons learned, as well as deeper understandings gained through this season? Of course, we use them for our own edification. But how about sharing this wisdom with others?

Regardless of your age, going through the death of a spouse, or any other deep, painful loss, will help you gain volumes of wisdom that many may never experience. Can you find joy in sharing this newfound understanding of God's ways with others? I would go so far as to say that one of the reasons God brought you through that desert was *so that* you could share what you've learned with others. It's putting purpose to your pain.

My ministry allows me to experience the joy of sharing my hard-learned lessons with others on a regular basis. Honestly, it's a "high" like few others I've encountered, all legal of course! But seriously, seeing someone's eyes light up when they grasp whatever concept God has laid on my heart to share is incredibly rewarding. Remember that we are God's hands and feet in this hurting world.

Have you learned anything about the importance of compassion? And how best to walk alongside someone who is hurting? Then be the friend that steps into their hurt with that understanding ear and open heart. The traditional definition of joy may not be what you impart to this friend, at least initially, but there is still an element of joy whenever you impart comfort.

Worth repeating – "Blessed be the God and Father of our Lord Jesus Christ, the Father of mercies and God of all comfort, who comforts us in all our affliction, so that we may be able to comfort those who are in any affliction, with the comfort with which we ourselves are comforted by God" (2 Corinthians 1:3-4).

This is a powerful opportunity to live out the scriptures and bring blessings into others' lives, and joy into your own. I strongly encourage you to take every opening God places in your path.

Life's Trajectory

One of the sayings I appreciate less and less through this season is, "Time heals all wounds." Not true. Time might heal some wounds, but some may remain as scabs throughout our lives. So I'm not naïve enough to expect every part of our widowed or shattered lives to eventually heal and be full of joy. Even without a major loss, I challenge you to find someone whose life has always been full of joy! Just not the nature of this fallen world in which we live.

That said, I do believe that time will allow some healing in our lives. And I *hope* there is more of that as the years go by. I want the waves to be fewer and farther between; I want the white of the egg to be so much bigger than the yolk, I want the ball to be so small that it seldom hits the pain button. In all the analogies we examined in Chapter 10, I want more healing and less pain.

Realistically, I don't expect every day to be less painful than the one before. This journey is hardly a straight line from heartache to healing. But I want to believe, despite the forever grief, that parts of my life will be more and more open to joy. God can't effectively use me if I'm stuck at the bottom of the pit, or still attending that pity party by myself.

It's a bit of a chicken and egg conundrum, isn't it? Make the effort to take that first step up the ladder and out of the pit, and then watch to see how God rewards you for trusting him. I understand that there are times we have no strength left to stand up, let alone start climbing up that ladder. But on the days when you feel God urging you forward, make your move. Then remember how good it felt to see that glimmer of sunshine and use *that* memory the next time you need to take another step of faith.

Often the only time we clearly see a positive trajectory is after years of struggle. Recent example from my life – I just commemorated my third birthday without Dale. It's one of those days that used to be full of joy and now is so often a reminder of who isn't here to celebrate with me. Sadness has been the primary emotion from this day, regardless of the good things I also enjoyed.

But this year was different. At the end of the day, I looked around my home and saw this: four beautiful flower arrangements, several of my favorite desserts, and a kitchen counter covered with birthday cards. Add to that about 130 birthday wishes on Facebook and multiple phone calls, texts, and Facetimes and I could only reach one conclusion.

This birthday was primarily *joyful*! Of course, I still missed Dale. I'm sad he wasn't here to give me his sweet card, and take me out to our favorite restaurant for dinner, and kiss me goodnight. But this was an exceptionally good day! I was blessed beyond my expectations.

And maybe most importantly, I noticed the difference between this birthday and the two previous ones. It felt like a milestone, of sorts. Finally, a "dreaded day" had become a "blessed day." God can and does bring joy into our lives during this season.

So, this is my hopeful expectation – God will continue to bring healing to my heart and allow joy to seep in ever so slowly, but purposefully. It is my prayer for all of you who are also grieving. Be patient. God is working.

The Hope of Heaven

If there is any theme that showed up again and again throughout this book, it's my longing for heaven and all that entails. It is the single greatest hope and joy I have as I walk through the heartache of widowhood. Of course, I want to see Dale again and the thought of that reunion sustains me through long days and nights. But even greater will be the joy of spending eternity in God's presence with Jesus at his right hand.

Here's how John described it in the book of Revelation:

> "Then I saw a new heaven and a new earth, for the first heaven and the first earth had passed away, and the sea was no more. And I saw the holy city, new Jerusalem, coming down out of heaven from God, prepared as a bride adorned for her husband. And I heard a loud voice from the throne saying, 'Behold, the dwelling place of God is with man. He will dwell with them, and they will be his people, and God himself will be with them as their God. He will wipe away every tear from their eyes, and death shall be no more, neither shall there be mourning, nor crying, nor pain anymore, for the former things have passed away.'
>
> "And he who was seated on the throne said, 'Behold, I am making all things new.' Also he said, 'Write this down, for these words are trustworthy and true.' And he said to me, 'It is done! I am the Alpha and the Omega, the beginning and the end. To the thirsty I will give from the spring of the water of life without payment. The one who conquers will have this heritage, and I will be his God and he will be my son'" (Revelation 21:1-7).

Some days it's all I can do to focus on the here and now. It seems that my heart is already there. This topic is so very present on my mind that I wrote a song recently that talked about my earthly heartache and my heavenly hope. Here are those words:

"I Long to See Your Face"

Words and Music by Lynne Hoeksema

Verse 1:

In the quiet of the evening, when all the shades are drawn.
My heart begins that journey, where together we belonged.
But now those days are over, and peace is hard to find.In
loneliness my heart cries and this thought fills my mind:

Chorus 1:

I long to see your face and put my hand in yours.
Embraced by your sweet love, together once more
Reliving happy times when life seemed, oh so fair.
So blessed by God's kind hand and underneath His care.

Verse 2:

I think about that future that seems so far away.
I picture you in heaven, perfection every day.
My mind sees our reunion as I run into your arms.
Hard years, they've disappeared now; we made it through the storms.

Chorus 2:

I long to see your face and put my hand in yours.
Embraced by your great love as we walk along the shore
In this perfect Promised Land where pain and tears are gone.
Our trials left behind; our love is now restored.

Bridge:

But I'm missing something vital in my view of heaven one day.
My focus is misguided so on my knees I pray,
"Forgive me, Lord, for putting my loved ones ahead of you.
We're here because of Jesus, his blood has made us new."
Yes, we are the created, and you - you are Creator God.
Why long for just the gift, when you're the giver of it all?
Hallelujah! Hallelujah! Hallelujah!

Chorus 3:

And when I see your face and put my hand in yours
Embraced by perfect love, now and forever more.
My longing will be o'er, my restless heart, be still.
My Savior, I am home, your promises fulfilled.
Hallelujah! Hallelujah! Amen!

That joy will be unlike anything we've ever experienced. When I tell people that I'm ready to go whenever God takes me, they often get a concerned look on their face and ask me, "Do you have a death wish?" To which I reply, "No, but I have a heaven wish!"

God will take me home on his timetable. And whether that's three days from now or thirty years, I want to serve him for whatever time I have left.

Whether you're reading this book as a fellow widow(er), as someone suffering through your own deep loss, or as an observer wanting to know more about the journey, I ask you the most important question in this book.

Do you know where you will spend eternity? Doesn't the description in Revelation sound "heavenly?" We have no idea!

So before closing out this story of *The Honest Griever*, I want to share the most important answer to that most important question. Here are the simple, but crucial steps to understanding what it means to be a true believer, and securing your place in heaven for eternity, compliments of the *Peaches & Prayer* website.[12]

1. The Truth: God

We were created by God, who is in control of everything. He created us to love, serve, and glorify him.

- Our all-powerful, holy God is in control of all of his creation (Genesis 1:1).
- He created us (Acts 17:25).
- He is always there watching over us; we cannot hide from him (Psalm 139:7-12).
- He formed us to serve him and only him (Matthew 4:10).
- All people and creation were made to glorify him (Romans 11:36).

2. The Truth: Sin

We are all sinners and are separated from God. We need to be restored to him.

- Our sins have separated us from God (Isaiah 59:1-2).

- We have all sinned and fallen short (Romans 3:23), and disregarded God's instructions and authority (Exodus 20:1-17; Matthew 22:37-40).
- We are unable to carry out good deeds because of our sinful nature (Romans 7:18).
- We are guilty of specific sins we have done or things we have not done, but should have (Psalms 32:1-5; 38:4).
- We need to be restored to God. We are wicked and are stuck in sin and have made God angry (Romans 1:18; 3:10-12). No one is righteous in God's sight (Romans 3:20).
- On our own, we do not have a way to eternal life. We have earned death because of our sins (Romans 6:23).

3. The Truth: Jesus

Only through Jesus Christ, the Son of God and Son of man, can people be restored to God.

- **Incarnation**: Jesus of Nazareth, who is God the Son, came to earth as a man to rescue sinners. His life on earth was free of sin (John 1:14; Colossians 1:19).
- **His Death**: Jesus' life's purpose was to die for mankind. He took our sins upon himself and accepted God's judgment with his death on the cross. God was satisfied with Jesus' death in our place. Jesus took the penalty for our sins with his death (John 1:29; Hebrews 9:27-28). Even when we were still sinners, Jesus died for our sins because God is full of grace and love (Romans 5:8).
- **His Resurrection**: God raised Jesus from the dead (Acts 2:24). In this, he showed he conquered sin and death through his obedience to God and his sinless life. His resurrection shows that God's wrath and penalty of sin were satisfied. Christ's triumph over the grave is heaven's pledge to us that we too shall be raised.
- **His Exaltation**: Jesus rose to heaven and is at the right hand of God. He is King and Lord of all (Hebrews 1:3; Matthew 28:18; Ephesians 1:20-21). He shares his righteousness with sinners who accept him as their Savior and Lord of their life. He gave his life to save all who acknowledge him (Hebrews 7:25).

4. The Truth: Man's Response

It is our response to have faith in Christ, repent for our sins and to seek God, and he will transform our lives.

- We are to trust and believe in Christ that he forgives sins. We have **faith** that we are going to heaven, that God has the power to transform our lives to glorify him. (Romans 12:1; Titus 3:4-7). Our new life will last an eternity (John 3:16). Faith is given to us by God (Ephesians 2:8).

- We **repent** as proof we have true faith. This changes our heart, mind, and our behavior. We learn to deny ourselves and decide to serve the LORD. (Romans 12:2; Titus 3:8) Our life is given for Christ. The LORD has the authority and right to expect anything from you.
- Our response to Christ's death is to die to sin and let him **transform** our lives for righteousness. Righteousness is possible by seeking the power of God. The Holy Spirit gives Christians the ability to think and live differently so we can please God (Romans 12:1-2; Ephesians 1:13-14, 19-20).

I hope and pray you will ask God to change your heart, if you're not already a believer in Jesus Christ. It's the most important decision of your life. Connect with me through my website, lynnehoeksema.com, if you want to talk further.

Thank you, from the bottom of this grateful heart, for walking alongside the journey of this "honest griever." I pray that you found my words helpful, hopeful, encouraging, validating, and ultimately joyful.

And so "the honest griever" culminates her story with the greatest Hope known to mankind.

Endnotes

1 http://www.loistonkin.com/
2 James 1:12
3 1 Peter 5:10
4 John 16:33
5 James 1:2-3
6 Romans 5:3-4
7 1 Peter 4:12-13
8 Romans 8:18
9 1 Peter 1:6-7
10 2 Corinthians 4:16-17
11 (Carol W. Cornish, *The Undistracted Widow – Living for God After Losing Your Husband,* Crossway, USA› p.37-38)
12 (Jenna, "4 Simple Steps to Sharing the Gospel in 30 Seconds," *Peaches & Prayer – A Crafty Christian Blog*, March 26, 2019, accessed May 17, 2020, https://peachesand-prayer.com/sharing-teh-gospel)

The Story Behind the Title

Now that you've reached the end of *The Honest Griever,* I'd like to divulge the story behind the title. Of course, I'd love for you to think that hours and hours of writing and tweaking and focus-group sessions went into this, but alas, it was a much simpler process. Here's the *truth* behind *The Honest Griever.*

I was doing a second interview with the local Christian radio station shortly after the publication of my first book. We were discussing the reasons why I wouldn't tell people I was doing "great" during those early months after Dale's death. I told her, first of all, I'm *not* doing great and secondly, why would I want to perpetuate the myth that I could be doing great a few months after the death of my husband of 31 years?

Then I said to her, "I want to be an honest griever." Something about that struck her as hilarious and she started laughing in the middle of this serious discussion! Actually, that's *exactly* when you need a good laugh, and I found her laughter contagious, so I was happy to join her in this little joke. Then she suggested, "We should put that on a mug!" To which I jokingly replied, "Or a book cover!" And immediately forgot about that exchange.

So as I began to think through this topic and what titles might represent it well, this conversation came to mind, and somehow it became the perfect fit.

My prayer is that you found not only an honest look at the heartache that descends upon someone as they become a widow or widower, but also the lessons and blessings and revelations from God that provide a healthy balance to that heartache.

I didn't want this to merely be a book where I dumped all my sad emotions on my readers. Yes, that is a part of it, but much more importantly, I hope you "honestly" saw the myriad and concrete ways that God walked alongside me on this journey from pain to purpose. And ultimately, see how he can do the same for you on your journey, wherever you are right now – and wherever God takes you.

About the Author

Lynne makes her home in Iowa, sharing space with Daisy and Winnie, her Boston Terrier/Frenchie mixes, and Max, the fearless cat. She spent nearly 25 years in the corporate world before retiring early to spend time with her husband, Dale.

After his death in October 2017, she founded the ministry *Be a Blessing to Your Grieving Friend.* And that is her goal – to teach others how to become the blessing their friends desperately need. She writes a weekly blog on her website, lynnehoeksema.com, sharing the wisdom she's learned through the pain of losing her husband.

She is the best-selling author of *Cultivating Compassion – Practical Advice as You Walk a Friend through a Season of Loss.* She is also a speaker and workshop leader, whose desire is to help others navigate the tricky waters of walking alongside someone who is grieving any kind of loss.

Lynne is active in her church, serving monthly on the worship team. She also loves being the piano accompanist for a great group of middle and high schoolers near their previous home.

lynnehoeksema.com

THANK YOU!

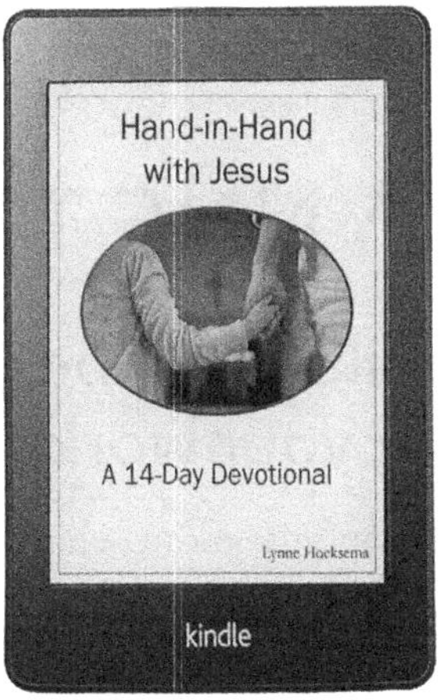

Hand-in-Hand with Jesus

A 14-Day Devotional

Thank you for reading *The Honest Griever*!

What can you learn on your walk with Jesus?

Looking for some practical applications?

In appreciation of your support,

please download this FREE PDF designed to do just that!

- Benefits of hanging onto Jesus' hand
- How to trust all his promises to us
- Who should and should not be on the walk with us
- How to overcome obstacles on our journey
- What should the pace of our walk be

Grab your FREE copy here:

lynnehoeksema.com/hand-in-hand-with-jesus-devotional

Best-selling Author of
Cultivating Compassion
Practical Advice as You Walk a Friend through a Season of Loss
Lynne Hoeksema

BOOK LYNNE TO SPEAK

Lynne is available to be your keynote speaker or your workshop leader.

Lynne speaks openly about what she experienced after the death of her husband of 31 years. Her "behind the scenes" perspective and practical knowledge will give you the confidence to step out in faith and bless someone in their time of need.

"We all 'mean well,' but just aren't sure how to show it. By sharing her own needs and wishes while she was grieving, the author generously and wisely advises the reader how to best comfort those who mourn. What a blessing. Thank you!"

"Lynne guides the reader with straightforward examples, and she gives testimony to the power of God to help both the griever and the comforter."

"Wow! Lynne offers so much in this quick read for those who really want to help a grieving friend. I have never read anything quite like it."

lynnehoeksema.com/speaking

lynne@lynnehoeksema.com

BE A BLESSING
TO YOUR GRIEVING FRIEND

PLEASE HELP!

Thanks so much for reading

The Honest Griever!

If you could spare just a few minutes,
I'd appreciate your honest re-
view on Amazon.com.

Just search for my book
and leave a brief review.

THANK YOU!!

Made in the USA
Las Vegas, NV
12 July 2022

51459024R00134